ALL THINGS
Meditations on Biblical Prayers for God's Help
ARE POSSIBLE

DANIEL PARTNER

BARBOUR
PUBLISHING

Published by Barbour Publishing, Inc., P.O. Box 719,
Uhrichsville, Ohio 44683, www.barbourbooks.com

Member of the
Evangelical Christian
Publishers Association

Printed in the United States of America.
5 4 3 2

ALL THINGS

Meditations on Biblical Prayers for God's Help

ARE POSSIBLE

For my children:
Darby, Brook, Promise, and Jeb

And the very God of peace sanctify you
wholly; and I pray God your whole spirit and
soul and body be preserved blameless unto the
coming of our Lord Jesus Christ.

INTRODUCTION

This book contains seventy-five prayers collected from the Bible. It begins with the very first prayer of Scripture: "Then began men to call upon the name of the Lord" (Genesis 4:26) and includes well-known prayers of the patriarchs and Moses, and even of Pharaoh. The Old Testament prophets are here, and we even look in on Jonah as he prays in the belly of a fish. You'll visit familiar figures such as Joshua, Deborah, Job, Hannah, her son Samuel, David the king, and other kings of ancient Israel.

Selections from the New Testament include three portions from the Lord's Prayer and prayers that Jesus himself offered to his God, including these weighty words, "My God, my God, why have you forsaken me?" (Matthew 27:46 NRSV). Prayers of Stephen and Paul are rich with meaning and encouragement and are included here. I tell of the self-righteous prayer of the Pharisee who felt he needed no help and the petition of the tax collector who thought he was beyond God's help. And I'll explain why, when speaking of prayer, Jesus asked, "When the Son of Man comes, will he find faith on earth?"

(Luke 18:8 NRSV). The last selection of *All Things Are Possible* is the final and ultimate prayer of the Bible: "Amen. Even so, come, Lord Jesus" (Revelation 22:20).

I have not drawn any prayers from the book of Psalms because Barbour Books recently released my book *I Give Myself to Prayer,* which is entirely concerned with the prayers of David and Solomon and other poets whose works are collected in the Psalms.

I treasure the truth of the gospel and the faith that is common to all believers in Christ and hope that you, the reader, feel the same way. I appreciate the advice of Jude, who wrote about our common salvation and appealed to us that we would only "contend for the faith that was once for all entrusted to the saints" (Jude 1:3 NRSV). That faith is not concerned with the minutia of doctrine, practice, or tradition. Instead, our faith glories in who God is, in the nature and person of Jesus Christ, in his exultant work of incarnation, redemption, and resurrection, and in the irrepressible hope of his Second Coming. These are the things all believers have in common. I write for people who believe them, and I want to help everyone enjoy this glorious gospel more and more.

As you read this book, I hope you sense that I respect your intelligence. I avoid patronizing my readers or telling them exactly what to do. After all, in the new covenant "They shall not. . . say to each other, 'Know the Lord,' for they shall all know me, from the least of them to the greatest" (Hebrews 8:11 NRSV).

The Bible is a living book, and I want to allow the scripture to breathe upon my readers and refresh them. The Lord is so living! He is much more alive than you or me. Let's labor together in hope that Christ will enlighten and enliven us, attract and even appear to us, as he did to the disciples at Emmaus (Luke 24:32).

No human problem is unique, yet God hears every believer's prayers. While you read *All Things Are Possible*, I hope you will see your own struggles in the prayers of biblical characters and be encouraged to lift your voice to heaven like the saints of old and truly embrace Jesus' promise: "All things are possible to him that believeth" (Mark 9:23).

DANIEL PARTNER
Sisters, Oregon
Summer 2002

DAY ONE

*And to Seth, to him also there was
born a son; and he called his name Enos:
then began men to call upon the
name of the Lord.*

GENESIS 4:26

The American author Walker Percy (1919–1990)
once said, "Christianity is so on target because at
the heart of it is the acknowledgment that man
has a problem; that man is in deep, deep trouble."

Our trouble had its beginning when the
primal couple, Adam and Eve, ate from the tree
of the knowledge of good and evil. Suddenly a
divide arose between them and their creator,
and they were expelled from the garden in
Eden. Humanity was cut off from all that God

could be to them and from all that God could do for them.

Formerly everything that grew in the garden was God's gift to Adam and Eve for food (Genesis 2:16). But outside the garden that supply was gone. They had to find their own food, so Cain became a farmer (4:3). In the garden they were naked (3:7), but without God they needed clothing, so Abel raised sheep (4:4). This is the way human culture began.

The tragic story of Cain's murder of Abel was man's next step away from the creator (4:1–16). And though the remainder of Genesis 4 seems to be a record of technological progress, it actually shows the growth of man's independence from God—the widening gap between the creature and the creator.

Whereas man had once found shelter in God, soon Jabal began to make tents. He also raised livestock to aid in laboring on the land (v. 20). His brother Jubal made music for enjoyment because the pleasure of God's presence was no more (v. 21). Tubal-cain was the first blacksmith, since he made tools of all kinds (v. 22). It seems that he also produced weapons, because men soon began to fight and kill each other (v. 23).

Man was in deep, deep trouble, so "then began men to call upon the name of the Lord" (v. 26). Someone, maybe Seth, realized that he had to get back to God and so called out to the Lord.

From that day to this, human culture has continued to develop unabated. Our independence from God is profound. But still it is true that "everyone who calls on the name of the Lord shall be saved" (Romans 10:13 NRSV).

*And he removed from thence unto
a mountain on the east of Bethel,
and pitched his tent, having Bethel on
the west, and Hai on the east: and
there he builded an altar unto the Lord,
and called upon the name of the Lord.*

GENESIS 12:8

I recently heard of a region in Louisiana where poverty is so extreme and deeply rooted that some children are utterly neglected. It is not unusual that they begin elementary school with no rudimentary knowledge. Not only do these children not know the alphabet, they don't know the names of colors. What is worse, teachers there have seen children who either have no

16

name or don't know what their name might be. This means that the teacher's first task is to teach the child his name. In other words, they have to build the person from scratch because, in a sense, a person without a name does not exist. Those children had seemingly never been called by name, so it is possible that no one had ever truly acknowledged their existence or communicated with them.

Abram called on the name of the Lord. In doing so, the father of faith taught us the way to acknowledge God's existence; the way to express faith; the way to worship and communicate with the Lord. Genesis 12:8 says that Abram built an altar, but it does not say that there was a sacrifice on that altar. It does not record a ceremony, a ritual, or a liturgy. It simply says that he called on the name of the Lord.

Did he kneel? Did he stand? Were his hands raised, or were they folded? No one knows; it is not important. What is known is that Abraham was in an extreme situation: "By faith Abraham, when he was called to go out into a place which he should after receive for an inheritance, obeyed; and he went out, not knowing whither he went.

By faith he sojourned in the land of promise, as in a strange country, dwelling in tabernacles with Isaac and Jacob, the heirs with him of the same promise" (Hebrews 11:8–9).

No amount of kneeling or crying or ceremony would help. And no other person could help. Abram's status, his knowledge, and his wisdom were of no use at this moment. But he knew God's name, so God existed for Abram. He called on the name of the Lord. This is the thing to do.

And Abram said, Lord God, what wilt thou give me, seeing I go childless, and the steward of my house is this Eliezer of Damascus? And Abram said, Behold, to me thou hast given no seed: and, lo, one born in my house is mine heir. And, behold, the word of the Lord came unto him, saying, This shall not be thine heir; but he that shall come forth out of thine own bowels shall be thine heir.

GENESIS 15:2–4

Abram was praying because he had a problem. God once told him that he would have a child that would inherit all the land of Canaan (Genesis 12:7). The problem was that Abram and his wife Sarai were much too old to have children.

In the prayer of Genesis 15:2–3, we overhear Abram telling God how to solve this problem: "What good are your blessings when I don't even have a son? Since this is the case, I want my servant Eliezer to inherit all my wealth. After all, you have given me no children, so one of my servants will have to be my heir." This is precisely how not to pray for God's help.

Abram's faith had not developed enough to enable him to patiently wait for God's answer to the problem, so he thought of a solution himself and prayed for God to accept it. God responded, "No. Eliezer will not be your heir. You will have a son of your own to inherit what I give you."

This illustrates why frustrations and dead ends sometimes appear in a believer's life. Do you recognize the following scenario? A problem comes up and an expedient solution springs to mind. Next, a prayer is offered in order to sanctify the idea. Finally, the solution is carried out. But often the results are not what were expected. This is called *living in the flesh;* the opposite is called *living by faith.*

The scene following Abram's fleshly prayer and God's patient response is so beautiful: "He brought him outside and said, 'Look toward heaven and count the stars, if you are able to count them' " (Genesis 15:5 NRSV).

When a problem arises or a decision must be made, you may want to remember how God and Abram stood together one night gazing up at the stars. If you do, pause with God; maybe step out the door and look up at the sky; whisper a prayer of faith—something like, "I believe in you." Then, like Abram, God will count you among the righteous (Genesis 15:6).

DAY FOUR

*And Abraham drew near, and said,
Wilt thou also destroy the righteous
with the wicked? Peradventure there
be fifty righteous within the city:
wilt thou also destroy and not spare
the place for the fifty righteous that are
therein? That be far from thee to do after
this manner, to slay the righteous with
the wicked: and that the righteous should
be as the wicked, that be far from thee:
Shall not the Judge of all
the earth do right?*

GENESIS 18:23–25

A remarkable event occurs in Genesis 18: God, accompanied by two angels, unexpectedly arrives at Abraham's camp in Mamre. Immediately, the father of faith hurries to wash their feet and serve them a generous meal. He stands nearby as they partake of the food in the shade of an old oak tree. As the three arise to leave, Abraham takes note that their eyes look away toward Sodom (v. 16), and immediately his heart goes out to his nephew Lot, who is living there. Abraham knows that the judgment and destruction of Sodom is near.

Lot seems to have had a knack for trouble. He had traveled with his uncle to Canaan from Chaldea (Genesis 11:31), which is now southern Iraq. Eventually, Lot's herdsmen came in conflict with those of Abraham, so the two separated, and Lot "settled among the cities of the Plain and moved his tent as far as Sodom" (13:12 NRSV). Though this was beautiful land (v. 10), Lot had made a bad decision because "the people of Sodom were wicked, great sinners against the Lord" (v. 13 NRSV).

Does your family include someone who has to be bailed out of difficulty from time to time? Lot was such a one. When he was kidnapped in the midst of the rebellion of the kings of Sodom and Gomorrah (14:1–12), Abraham rose up with 318 men and rescued his nephew (vv. 13–16). Delivered from that tight spot, Lot made another bad decision and returned to live in Sodom. Little did he know that two angels were headed his way to carry out God's judgment (18:22).

Abraham, who loved Lot, knew what was to occur and prayed in a way that saved his nephew from dying in the destruction of Sodom. This prayer is seen in Genesis 18:23–33 (NRSV). In it, Abraham does not even mention the beloved Lot. Instead he invokes what is important to God—"Shall not the Judge of all the earth do what is just?" (v. 25). This, with the rest of the prayer, reminded God that divine righteousness requires the salvation of those who believe. To do otherwise would be unjust. God was convinced, and Lot was saved.

Abraham put aside his strong personal feelings for his nephew and focused his prayer on God, whose judgment is righteous. In this way the Scripture shows us that an effective prayer is one that is spoken according to who God is.

*And the Lord appeared unto him
the same night, and said,
I am the God of Abraham thy father:
fear not, for I am with thee, and will bless
thee, and multiply thy seed for my servant
Abraham's sake. And he built an altar
there, and called upon the name of
the Lord, and pitched his tent there:
and there Isaac's servants digged a well.*

GENESIS 26:24–25

I once served at a polling place in Old Saybrook, Connecticut. I sat at a table and checked names off a master list of registered voters as people arrived to vote in the presidential election. Everybody in the district who wanted to vote came to the table and gave their name. It so happens that the actress Katharine Hepburn lives in Old Saybrook. In those days, nearly everyone in town recognized Ms. Hepburn. They knew where she lived and where she shopped; some even greeted her by name. Naturally, she came to vote that day, and no matter how famous she was, she still had to identify herself so I could check her name off the list.

In Genesis 26, God came to Isaac and identified himself: "I am the God of Abraham thy father." Isaac then did the identical things his father had done years before: He built an altar and called on the name of the Lord.

This event is a model for us. Jesus may be the most famous person who ever lived, but he has to introduce himself to each individual who comes to believe in him.

For example, I know a woman who was raised attending church, Sunday school, youth group, church camp—the works. Plus, she attended a Christian college and two seminaries, receiving a graduate degree in theology. She served in churches for many years. Then two things happened. She visited missions in Africa, where she met people for whom Christ was real, a living presence each day; and her father died.

At this juncture, Jesus introduced himself: "I am God." This dear woman responded like Job, "I had heard of you by the hearing of the ear, but now my eye sees you" (Job 42:5 NRSV), and she called on the name of the Lord. God was true to his word, and she was saved (Romans 10:13).

Likewise, Isaac was raised by Abraham, the father of faith, but this was not enough to secure for Isaac a life of faith. God had to personally introduce himself before Isaac called on the name of the Lord. Such an introduction can come in many ways. Often, it is in the midst of affliction when Jesus introduces himself; he shakes your hand, touches on your shoulder, and says, "Hello, I am God."

*And Jacob said, O God of my father
Abraham, and God of my father Isaac,
the Lord which saidst unto me,
Return unto thy country, and to thy
kindred, and I will deal well with thee:
I am not worthy of the least of all the
mercies, and of all the truth, which thou
hast shewed unto thy servant; for with
my staff I passed over this Jordan;
and now I am become two bands.*

GENESIS 32:9–10

Jacob knows God, to whom he prays; he knows
the words that God has spoken; he knows what
are the merciful things God has done for him. In
other words, Jacob knows the truth and so, in his

praying, teaches us how to pray.

First, Jacob calls God by name—"O God of my father Abraham, and God of my father Isaac." What intimacy! God had become a member of Jacob's family. Plus, his family was fully identified by their relationship with God. What a family it was!—Abraham and Sarah; Isaac and Rebekah; Jacob and his beloved Rachel with her sons, Joseph and Benjamin; Leah, Bilhah, and Zilpah, the mothers of Jacob's ten other sons; plus Leah's daughter Dinah. All these bring to mind the one God who is intimately involved with humanity, the God of Abraham, Isaac, and Jacob.

Still today we can pray to the "Father from whom every family in heaven and on earth takes its name" (Ephesians 3:14–15 NRSV). Although I am not quite sure what this means, when I use this phrase in prayer, I am certain that my family has been named by the very God who is also the "God of our Lord Jesus Christ, the Father of glory" (Ephesians 1:17).

Jacob called out in prayer, "O God of *my* father." How possessive! He and his parents had experienced God to the extent that God belonged to them. Thousands of years later, the apostle Paul prayed in this same way, saying, "I thank *my* God upon every remembrance of you" (Philippians 1:3).

Only two people in the New Testament referred to God as "my God." These people are Jesus Christ and Paul the Apostle, although one exception is seen in John 20:17. "Jesus saith unto her, Touch me not; for I am not yet ascended to my Father: but go to my brethren, and say unto them, I ascend unto my Father, and your Father; and to my God, and your God." These first words of the resurrected Christ are potent evidence that now, through the crucifixion and resurrection, God can be possessed by everyone.

So be sure that God does not only belong to someone else in your life—to a pastor, a friend, or a family member. God is *your God* as well. After all, this is the age of the new covenant when "all shall know me, from the least to the greatest" (Hebrews 8:11).

*And Jacob said, O God of my father
Abraham, and God of my father Isaac,
the Lord which saidst unto me,
Return unto thy country, and to thy
kindred, and I will deal well with thee:
I am not worthy of the least of all the
mercies, and of all the truth, which thou
hast shewed unto thy servant; for with
my staff I passed over this Jordan;
and now I am become two bands.*

GENESIS 32:9–10

Let us continue to consider this prayer. Jacob is intimate with the God of his family and possessive of God, just like Paul, who prayed, "I thank my God" (Philippians 1:3).

Next Jacob becomes audacious, praying, "O Lord who said to me, 'Return to your country and to your kindred, and I will do you good'" (Genesis 32:9 NRSV). He is challenging God to fulfill this promise; he wants to be sure that God remembers the words, "I will do you good."

I believe that the best way to pray is to audaciously use the words of the Bible. Do you need strength? I often adapt Ephesians 3:16 to pray for this: "According to the riches of your glory, dear God, grant that I may be strengthened in my inner being with power through your Spirit, and that Christ may dwell in my heart through faith as I am being rooted and grounded in love."

Do you enjoy the wonders of God's creation? Colossians 1:15–17 lends words to a prayer of thanksgiving for this: "Oh Lord Jesus Christ, you are the image of the invisible God, the firstborn of all creation. All things in heaven and on earth were created in you—the things that I can see and the things that I cannot see; even thrones and dominions and rulers and powers— all things have been created through you and for you. And you yourself are before all things, and in you all things hold together."

While using the words of Scripture to enrich and empower prayer, we become mindful, like Jacob, "of all the mercies, and of all the truth, which thou hast shewed unto thy servant" (Genesis 32:10). These mercies and this truth are encapsulated in the Bible. Its use in prayer lends eloquence and great meaning to our supplication. When God's mercies and truth are the content of prayer, both the believer and the one in whom we believe are reminded of all that has been accomplished from the creation through the redemption to the end of the age.

*And Moses said unto God, Who am I,
that I should go unto Pharaoh,
and that I should bring forth
the children of Israel out of Egypt?
And he said, Certainly I will be with thee;
and this shall be a token unto thee,
that I have sent thee: When thou hast
brought forth the people out of Egypt,
ye shall serve God upon this mountain.*

EXODUS 3:11–12

People are interested in answered prayer. I've read
of believers who keep records of their prayers,
including the dates when the answers arrived.
Some who are critical of the faith that causes
folks to pray point out that many prayers never

seem to be answered. Others have said that God's answer to most petitions is *no*. But Moses, in his interaction with God at the burning bush, illustrates that unanswered prayers can be a result of asking for the wrong thing.

"Who am I," asks Moses, "that I should go unto Pharaoh, and that I should bring forth the children of Israel out of Egypt?" This is a very good question, although Moses already knew what he was—the adopted son of Pharaoh's daughter and a murderer who, decades earlier, fled from Egypt, married the daughter of the priest of Midian, and became a shepherd on the backside of the desert (Exodus 2:11–3:1). He himself said, "I have been a stranger in a strange land" (2:22).

No wonder Moses was surprised that God would tell him, "So come, I will send you to Pharaoh to bring my people, the Israelites, out of Egypt" (3:10 NRSV). Certainly he felt inadequate for this responsibility, so Moses asked, "Who am I, that I should go unto Pharaoh?" Even at that marvelous burning bush, Moses could not help but pray for himself. His prayer was not answered; instead, he was mercifully refocused on the one he needed in that moment and always: "Certainly I will be with thee," said God.

The focus of the faith is not oneself. It is God, especially God in Christ. The primary purpose of the Bible is to reveal God and God's purpose to men and women of every generation. This is the way the apostle Paul prayed for us: "That the God of our Lord Jesus Christ, the Father of glory, may give unto you the spirit of wisdom and revelation in the knowledge of him: The eyes of your understanding being enlightened; that ye may know what is the hope of his calling, and what the riches of the glory of his inheritance in the saints" (Ephesians 1:17–18).

Pray out of your desire to know the Lord. Such prayers are answered.

DAY NINE

And Moses said unto God, Behold,
when I come unto the children of Israel,
and shall say unto them, The God of your
fathers hath sent me unto you; and they
shall say to me, What is his name?
what shall I say unto them?
And God said unto Moses,
I AM THAT I AM: and he said,
Thus shalt thou say unto the children of
Israel, I AM hath sent me unto you.

EXODUS 3:13–14

Why are we living? This great question of the
ages is answered in the Bible: "From one ancestor
[God] made all nations to inhabit the whole
earth, and he allotted the times of their existence

and the boundaries of the places where they would live, so that they would search for God and perhaps grope for him and find him— though indeed he is not far from each one of us" (Acts 17:26–27 NRSV).

We are here to search, even grope, for God, though not in a vain, endless search; our life purpose is to find God. This is not difficult, since "indeed he is not far from each one of us."

I searched and groped for God, though all my life I had never really prayed. My parents did teach me to pray before I went to bed: "Now I lay me down to sleep, I pray the Lord my soul to keep, and if I die before I wake, I pray the Lord my soul to take." But I grew up and left that prayer behind with my toy trucks. In pondering the meaning of existence and the identity of God, I read many books and engaged in conversation with anyone who was willing to talk about the problem. Through my reading, I eventually realized there was one thing I hadn't tried. I hadn't prayed.

Even though I didn't know any pattern or way of prayer, I began to pray. As I passed through my days, I would occasionally stop and say, "God, I want to know you." That was all. This was in the days when many churches were open during the day so people could drop in for personal prayer. If I had time when passing by a church or chapel, I would go in, sit for awhile, say, "God, I want to know you," and then go on my way.

Little did I know it at the time, but this is exactly how the search for God is accomplished. Moses himself shows us this way. He was in circumstances so extraordinary that none of us will ever see such a thing. He encountered God as a flame in a bush on a mountainside in a Middle Eastern desert. There he asked a very ordinary question, a question that every person can ask of God: "Who are you?"

God answered my question in Christ, and since that day I've known that "indeed he is not far from each one of us."

DAY TEN

*Then Pharaoh called for Moses and Aaron,
and said, Intreat the Lord, that he may
take away the frogs from me, and from
my people; and I will let the people go,
that they may do sacrifice unto the Lord.*

EXODUS 8:8

When my oldest daughter was about four years old, we had a little pond out back in which lived a generous population of bullfrogs. These frogs were large, careful, and quick, and my daughter could catch them better than anyone in the neighborhood. Boys would stand aside and marvel at her frog-snatching technique. Sometimes a half-dozen or more frogs would spend an afternoon imprisoned in our bathtub until set free to be caught again another day. Every once in awhile, an accident would happen to one of these amphibian captives. This is why I know that a dead bullfrog is fairly disgusting. And to think that Egypt was once utterly filled with dead frogs.

This happened because Pharaoh would not release the children of Israel from bondage. So, on God's instruction, Aaron pointed his shepherd's staff toward the rivers, canals, and marshes of Egypt, and a horrendous plague of frogs covered the entire countryside. In this incomprehensible calamity, Pharaoh no doubt asked his wizards to pray or work some magic to cause the frogs to go away. But the wizards had no power for this, so Pharaoh asked Moses to pray, and the frogs "in the houses, the court-yards, and the fields" all died. They were piled into great heaps, "and the land stank" (Exodus 8:13–14 NRSV).

Pharaoh is one of the great villains of the Bible, so it is hard to have any sympathy for him. But this great villain had a great big problem: God had filled his country with frogs. He had no power to deal with this, so he turned to prayer, and the way he prayed was to have someone else do it for him. It was remarkable that Pharaoh requested prayer. He knew that only the God of the Israelites could help him.

I think that we should count this as a valid way to pray—the way of people who cannot pray on their own. They may be hardened toward God or unrepentant. Pride or grief may have muted their heart's cry. Also, any one of us could become physically weak or in pain and so unable to pray. Then we would know that the impulse to ask for prayer is itself a turning toward God. This is truly prayer. As the old hymn says:

Prayer is the soul's sincere desire,
Uttered, or unexpressed;
The motion of a hidden fire
That trembles in the breast.

Prayer is the burden of a sigh,
The falling of a tear;
The upward glancing of an eye
When none but God is near.

James Montgomery (1771–1854).

*Speak ye unto all the congregation
of Israel, saying, In the tenth day of this
month they shall take to them every man
a lamb, according to the house of their
fathers, a lamb for an house. . . . And they
shall take of the blood, and strike it on the
two side posts and on the upper door post
of the houses, wherein they shall eat it.*

EXODUS 12:3, 7

On the night of the Passover, blood was the
only thing that distinguished the houses of the
Israelites from the houses of the Egyptians.
Doubtless, there were many differences between
these two races, but only the blood of the
Passover lamb secured all the firstborn of Israel

from the sword of the destroying angel (Exodus 12:12–13).

Likewise, a Christian family may be very different from others in its appearance, activities, and attitudes. These things, though very good, do not speak to God. The blood of the Lamb of God is a Christian's most eloquent, most powerful prayer.

"Prayer?" you may say. "How can Jesus' blood be a prayer?"

The new covenant is ratified by the blood of Christ the redeemer. It is sprinkled upon our consciences just as the blood of the old covenant sacrifice was sprinkled upon the altar (Hebrews 10:22). This blood pacifies God and purifies the consciences of believing men and women.

Jesus' blood is prayer because it is speaking blood. This is seen in Hebrews 12:24, which says that believers have come "to Jesus the mediator of the new covenant, and to the blood of sprinkling, that speaketh better things than that of Abel."

The blood of Abel cried out to God from the ground, pleading for vengeance upon Cain (Genesis 4:10). Though we are as guilty as

Cain, Jesus' blood doesn't plead for retribution but for mercy. It speaks to us sinners in the name of God, telling of pardon for our sins and peace to our souls. Finally, as we claim the blood's effectiveness, it utters the ineffable—our obedience to the gospel and our highest love and thankfulness to God.

Mercy, pardon, peace, obedience, love, thanksgiving—these are the prayers of the blood of Christ. So we sing:

Paschal Lamb, by God appointed,
all our sins on thee were laid;
By our Father's love anointed,
thou redemption's price hast paid.
All who trust thee are forgiven
Through the virtue of thy blood;
Opened are the things of heaven,
Grace shines forth to man from God.

John Bakewell (1721–1819).

Day Twelve

And Moses returned unto the Lord,
and said, Oh, this people have sinned
a great sin, and have made
them gods of gold.
Yet now, if thou wilt forgive their sin—;
and if not, blot me, I pray thee,
out of thy book which thou hast written.

EXODUS 32:31–32

When my son was about ten years old, he decided to lead his friends in smashing jack-o'-lanterns at Halloween. He did the wrong thing; yet when he was caught, I was there immediately to be sure he was treated justly. I have found that often no one will argue a mischievous boy's case, whether in school or in the neighborhood. A father must be his son's advocate.

Moses often had to advocate for the children of Israel. The crisis of the golden calf was extreme, and Moses was so desperate that he was willing to substitute for the Israelites in God's punishment. I have experienced this same impulse. With each of my children I have at some time wished that I could take their place so they would not have to suffer. But this is not possible. Not even Moses could do it.

However, these days we have one advantage over Moses in this matter: Everything changed at about three o'clock on the afternoon of Christ's death. Then Christ cried out in agony, "My God, my God, why hast thou forsaken me?" (Matthew 27:46). On that cross, God made Christ "to be sin for us, who knew no sin; that we might be made the righteousness of God in him" (2 Corinthians 5:21).

In the hours of his death on the cross, Jesus accomplished what no one had ever done and never again will do. He became the substitute in God's judgment—not for just one person, but for all people: "He has appeared once *for all* at the end of the age to remove sin by the sacrifice of himself (Hebrews 9:26 NRSV, italics added).

We cannot ourselves substitute for those we love, those who are in trouble or suffering, but we can forcefully advocate for them in prayer, based on Christ's ultimate act of love. It is our most powerful appeal in prayer: "Lord, you loved her so much that you died for her under God's judgment. So please go to her now in love, comfort her as she suffers, and draw her to yourself."

And Moses said unto the Lord, See, thou sayest unto me, Bring up this people: and thou hast not let me know whom thou wilt send with me. Yet thou hast said, I know thee by name, and thou hast also found grace in my sight. Now therefore, I pray thee, if I have found grace in thy sight, shew me now thy way, that I may know thee, that I may find grace in thy sight: and consider that this nation is thy people. And he said, My presence shall go with thee, and I will give thee rest.

EXODUS 33:12–14

Over and over again, the apostles express the desire that Christ's believers would have grace.

"Grace to you," wrote Paul. "Grace and peace be yours in abundance," said Peter (1 Corinthians 1:3; 2 Peter 1:2 NRSV). Their job was to announce the good news that the Word became flesh and lived among us full of grace (John 1:14 NRSV). Grace is central to the gospel, so much so that the gospel is condensed in one sentence: "The law indeed was given through Moses; grace and truth came through Jesus Christ" (v. 17 NRSV).

Though Moses is best known as the law-giver, he also found grace with God. His prayer tells us what grace was to him and what it can be to us. "If I have found grace in thy sight, shew me now thy way, that I may know thee" (Exodus 33:13). Grace is to know the Lord's way and, even more, to know the Lord.

For Moses and Israel, the Lord's way was the road they would follow through the wilderness and into the Good Land. For us, it is the way of salvation (Acts 16:17). If you know this way, you know God's grace.

The way is Jesus Christ, who said, "I am the way. . . No one comes to the Father except through me" (John 14:6 NRSV). The way of salvation is the path of Christ's life. He was

God born as an actual man, the same in every way as you and me, except he had no sin. He lived a perfect life, suffered crucifixion, was certified dead, and buried in the earth. Then he rose from death, destroying its power, and ascended to heaven in triumph. This was the way Jesus traveled through his life. To know the way Christ traveled is to have grace.

The New Testament tells of the single step you and I must take on the way of salvation: "Believe on the Lord Jesus, and you will be saved" (Acts 16:31 NRSV). Christ has already traveled the way for us, and there is nothing left for anyone to do except believe in him. This act of believing is grace as well.

DAY FOURTEEN

And thou shalt make an altar to burn incense upon. . . . And Aaron shall burn thereon sweet incense every morning: when he dresseth the lamps, he shall burn incense upon it. And when Aaron lighteth the lamps at even, he shall burn incense upon it, a perpetual incense before the Lord throughout your generations.

EXODUS 30:1, 7–8

Prayer is the real incense. Its fragrance can suffuse a believer's life. "Let my prayer be set forth before thee as incense; and the lifting up of my hands as the evening sacrifice" (Psalm 141:2). Morning and evening, Aaron burned incense in the tabernacle, a ritual that became known as the time of incense when "the whole multitude of the people were praying" (Luke 1:9–10).

Let's not ignore the fact that the Bible likens prayer to incense: "And another angel came. . .and there was given unto him much incense, that he should offer it with the prayers of all saints upon the golden altar which was before the throne. And the smoke of the incense, which came with the prayers of the saints, ascended up before God out of the angel's hand" (Revelation 8:3–4).

I've often wondered how to follow the New Testament's instruction to "pray without ceasing" (1 Thessalonians 5:17). Now I think that it is something like "a perpetual incense before the Lord." Aaron's way was to burn incense morning and evening, and God called this a perpetual incense. If you and I prayed morning and evening year after year, would God call this "perpetual prayer"? It is worth a try. Just as the scent of incense lingers far past the time of its burning, the effect of morning prayer can last through the day and the fragrance of evening prayer can remain until sunrise.

Liturgical churches, those churches whose

worship centers on ritual, have been practicing such prayer for centuries. They call it the Liturgy of the Hours or the Divine Office. This rich resource provides prayers, psalms, and meditation not only for morning and evening, but for every hour of every day. All over the world, hundreds of thousands of believers pray the Divine Office daily in public and in private, in kitchens and cathedrals, palaces and prisons.

These folks' prayers are strengthened by the liturgy. Your prayers may be guided by your daily devotional readings. However prayer is practiced, it is like incense. While sound in the ears can be shut off and one's eyes can look away, the long-lasting fragrance of prayer cannot be ignored.

*And the priest shall put some of the blood
upon the horns of the altar of
sweet incense before the Lord,
which is in the tabernacle of the
congregation; and shall pour
all the blood of the bullock at the bottom
of the altar of the burnt offering,
which is at the door of the tabernacle
of the congregation.*

LEVITICUS 4:7

What do you think prevents you from praying?
Here are three possibilities: You don't have the
time; you don't have the faith; you don't have the
words. But remember, you do have the blood of
Christ. These problems will evaporate if you do

one thing—put some of the blood on the horns of the altar of sweet incense. In other words, let the first topic of prayer be the cleansing of your sin. It is sin that prevents prayer.

You have the blood of the everlasting covenant (Hebrews 13:20) in which God promises, "[Your] sins and iniquities will I remember no more" (10:17). The problem is, although God forgets your sins, you can't. Before you can truly pray, your conscience must be cleansed by "the blood of Christ, who through the eternal Spirit offered himself without spot to God." This will "purge your conscience. . .to serve the living God" (Hebrews 9:14).

To know Jesus Christ is to know his blood. It may take practice to learn to enjoy the cleansing by the Lord's blood, but this is the way to partake of the benefits of his redemption. Not the least of these is the "boldness to enter into the holiest by the blood of Jesus, by a new and living way, which he hath consecrated for us" (Hebrews 10:19–20).

It's as simple as that. Every day, the ancient Jewish priests took some of the blood of the sin offering into the Tabernacle and put it on the incense altar, the place of prayer. In this day and age, we take the blood of Christ, by faith put it upon our heart, and enter the door of prayer.

*And Nadab and Abihu, the sons of Aaron,
took either of them his censer, and
put fire therein, and put incense thereon,
and offered strange fire before the Lord,
which he commanded them not.
And there went out fire from the Lord,
and devoured them,
and they died before the Lord.*

LEVITICUS 10:1–2

I present the frightening story of Nadab and
Abihu because it offers a simple warning. As
with all Scripture, I hope the reader will apply it
only to herself, only to himself, not to others.

These two men were sons of the high priest,
Aaron. They too were priests whose duties

included the offering of incense. But they were presumptuous, brazen, out of order; they offered incense without God's command, without divine permission.

Since the Bible likens the burning of incense to the offering of prayer (see Psalm 141:2), this is where we can apply the lesson of the story of Nadab and Abihu: Don't run ahead of the Lord in your prayer. There may be many things that you want to do for the Lord and many more things that you want the Lord to do for you. Before praying for these things, ask this question: Has God commanded me to burn this incense? And remember the Lord's warning:

Not every one that saith unto me, Lord, Lord, shall enter into the kingdom of heaven; but he that doeth the will of my Father which is in heaven. Many will say to me in that day, Lord, Lord, have we not prophesied in thy name? and in thy name have cast out devils? and in thy name done many wonderful works? And then will I profess unto them, I

never knew you: depart from me, ye that
work iniquity. (Matthew 7:21–23)

Out of all the prayers that are offered every
day, how many express the will of the Father? I
cannot answer that question. But if Nadab and
Abihu were here, I think they would advise us
all to seek God's permission before we fill our
censer with the incense of good ideas. If not,
though fire won't fall from heaven, our prayers
will be dead.

It may be best to begin to pray with the
confession that you don't know what you should
pray for, or how you should pray. Ask the Holy
Spirit to pray for you with groanings that cannot
be expressed in words. Because the Scripture
assures that "God, who searches the heart, knows
what is the mind of the Spirit, because the Spirit
intercedes for the saints according to the will of
God" (Romans 8:26–27 NRSV).

Day Seventeen

*And the Lord spake unto Moses, saying,
Speak unto Aaron and unto his sons,
saying, On this wise ye shall bless the
children of Israel, saying unto them,
The Lord bless thee, and keep thee:
The Lord make his face shine upon thee,
and be gracious unto thee: The Lord lift up
his countenance upon thee, and give thee
peace. And they shall put my name upon
the children of Israel; and I will bless them.*

NUMBERS 6:22–27

I don't recall ever writing to Santa Claus. I think
I just told my parents about the gifts I hoped to
receive at Christmas. How else could they know
a little boy's desires? I remember the Christmas

morning thrill of finding an entire army of tiny plastic soldiers carefully set in battle array. It was exactly what I'd asked for. It may have been the same Christmas that I got my first book—as requested—*The Adventures of Robin Hood.*

Much prayer is spent telling God that we want various blessings such as prosperity, health, safety, and friendship. But God is not Santa Claus. Despite what we may want, the above verses from Numbers describe the way God prefers to bless us. What Christian does not know "God so loved the world, that he gave his only begotten Son" (John 3:16). Therefore, it should come as no surprise that God wants to bless us with himself.

Notice that the name *Lord* is repeated three times in this blessing. This expresses the great mystery of the Godhead—who is three and yet one God: The Father to bless and keep us; the Son to be gracious to us; and the Holy Spirit to give us peace. The true blessing is the Triune God. God is the real prosperity, health, safety, and friendship. What more is needed? The apostle Paul blessed us with the same Triune God: "The grace of the Lord Jesus Christ, the love of

God, and the communion of the Holy Spirit be with all of you" (2 Corinthians 13:13 NRSV).

The evangelist, preacher, and hymnist A. B. Simpson (1843–1919) founded the Christian and Missionary Alliance. He knew that God is all a Christian truly needs. One of my favorite hymns by Simpson begins this way:

> Once it was the blessing,
> Now it is the Lord;
> Once it was the feeling,
> Now it is his Word;
> Once his gift I wanted,
> Now, the giver own;
> Once I sought for healing,
> Now himself alone.

DAY EIGHTEEN

*And it came to pass, when the ark set
forward, that Moses said, Rise up, Lord,
and let thine enemies be scattered;
and let them that hate thee flee before thee.
And when it rested, he said, Return,
O Lord, unto the many thousands of Israel.*

NUMBERS 10:35–36

Every day is a journey. It begins in the morning the moment your feet touch the floor at your bedside. When you lift them into bed again, the journey is over, and you rest. Most days, my journey doesn't take me far. In fact, I go in a circle from my home office, ten miles into town for my mail and other errands, and home again. Usually, nothing out of the ordinary happens. Maybe I'll see a friend and stop to chat; recently, my front driver's side tire went flat in the parking lot at the grocery store. Pretty boring. Nothing like the journey of Israel's multitude in the Sinai.

At that time, Moses uttered a prayer on behalf of the people both at the commencement and the end of each day. All of Israel's historic journeys were sanctified by devotion, and so should ours be, no matter how ordinary.

The simplicity of Moses' prayers show that morning and evening prayers don't need to be fancy. "Rise up, Lord," he says, "and let thine enemies be scattered." This shows that our morning prayer is about what has been accomplished. Christ scattered his enemies in crucifixion when he "spoiled principalities and powers" (Colossians 2:15), and in resurrection when he defeated death (1 Corinthians 15:20), and in ascension when "he led captivity captive" (Ephesians 4:8). Prayers of thanksgiving to God for the work Christ has done are a strong underpinning for each day.

Then evening comes. The day has passed, and, again, it was not the day of Christ's promised return (Acts 1:11). The evening prayer is one of hope in the work Christ has yet to do: "Return, O Lord," prays Moses. This, I believe, is the consummate prayer; it is the Bible's final prayer: "He which testifieth these things saith, Surely I come quickly. Amen. Even so, come, Lord Jesus" (Revelation 22:20).

*Thus I fell down before the Lord forty days
and forty nights, as I fell down at the first;
because the Lord had said he would
destroy you. I prayed therefore unto the
Lord, and said, O Lord God, destroy
not thy people and thine inheritance,
which thou hast redeemed through
thy greatness, which thou hast brought
forth out of Egypt with a mighty hand.*

DEUTERONOMY 9:25–26

This is a prayer that really worked.

The situation was this: At Kadesh-barnea the people of Israel refused to go into the promised land despite God's command to do so. So God responded: "I will smite them with the pestilence, and disinherit them, and will make of thee [Moses] a greater nation and mightier than they" (Numbers 14:12). At that time, Moses prayed the above prayer.

Clearly, God did not destroy Israel. The question is, why did God do as Moses asked? To know this may help us pray more effectively.

Moses first reminded God of the work that had already been done: "Thou hast redeemed [Israel] through thy greatness," bringing them "out of Egypt with a mighty hand." Next Moses reminded God of the promises: "Remember thy servants, Abraham, Isaac, and Jacob" (Deuteronomy 9:27). These were the men who received the promise that Abraham's offspring would inherit the land of Canaan (Genesis 17:7–8). Then Moses reminded God of the testimony: "Lest the land whence thou broughtest us out say. . .he hath brought them out to slay them in the wilderness" (Deuteronomy 9:28).

God's work, God's promises, God's testimony. Instill your prayers with these.

The work that we Christians remember in prayer is summed up in four words— incarnation, crucifixion, resurrection, ascension.

This work of Christ is the topic of nearly all the New Testament: God was born in humanity, died for redemption, was resurrected in triumph, and ascended into glory! This is enough to fill every prayer until the end.

And the promises! For the present time these are yours: the Holy Spirit of promise (Ephesians 1:13), the promise of life which is in Christ Jesus (2 Timothy 1:1), and the promise of entering into God's rest (Hebrews 4:1). In the future, you will have eternal life, promised before the world began (Titus 1:2), the promise of eternal inheritance (Hebrews 9:15), and the kingdom with "the crown of life, which the Lord hath promised to them that love him" (James 1:12; 2:5). A powerful prayer, which is an answered prayer, reminds God of these promises.

Such prayer upholds God's testimony, making "everyone see what is the plan of the mystery hidden for ages in God. . .so that through the church the wisdom of God in its rich variety might now be made known. . .in accordance with the eternal purpose that he has carried out in Christ Jesus our Lord" (Ephesians 3:9–11 NRSV).

DAY TWENTY

*Then spake Joshua to the Lord in the day
when the Lord delivered up the Amorites
before the children of Israel, and he said in
the sight of Israel, Sun, stand thou still
upon Gibeon; and thou, Moon, in the
valley of Ajalon. And the sun stood still,
and the moon stayed, until the people had
avenged themselves upon their enemies.
Is not this written in the book of Jasher?
So the sun stood still in the midst of
heaven, and hasted not to go down
about a whole day.*

JOSHUA 10:12–13

Here the author of the book of Joshua breaks
away from his story to interpose an ancient

song found in the book of Jasher. No copies of this book exist anymore. It apparently was a collection of songs honoring Israel's national heroes. The Song of the Bow, another portion of the book of Jasher, is found in 2 Samuel 1:17–27. Here, Jasher's poem commemorates one of the mighty acts of Joshua.

Notice that the poem personifies the sun and moon; they are addressed as intelligent beings. This is very poetic. It is interesting to note that before about 1870, when Christian theologians began to do battle with the advocates of Darwin's theory of evolution, orthodox Bible commentators had no problem seeing this as a poem. It is poetic to say that the sun stood still and the moon stopped. But did they? Some explained that the light of the sun was indeed supernaturally prolonged, but this was accomplished by the physical laws of refraction and reflection that still today can cause the sun to appear above the horizon when it is actually below it.

Modern advocates of Creationism say that this event cannot and must not be explained scientifically, much less poetically. The creator, they say, is perfectly capable of violating the laws of physics. God can and did stop the movements of the earth and moon without causing the cosmos to crash.

I have one problem with this epic struggle between religion and science: "I am afraid that as the serpent deceived Eve by its cunning, your thoughts will be led astray from a sincere and pure devotion to Christ" (2 Corinthians 11:3 NRSV). Ramming this portion of Joshua into the musket of Creationism robs us of the inspiring lesson Jasher hoped to impart.

This Scripture is not about God the creator; it is about Joshua, the man of faith who had marched all night and fought all day. One might expect him to want a little sleep and give his army some time to rest. Instead, he wanted to prolong the day. He wanted to complete his work and defeat "the whole land, the hill country and the Negeb and the lowland and the slopes, and all their kings. . .as the Lord God of Israel commanded" (Joshua 10:40 NRSV). This desire caused great faith to arise in Joshua, who believed the power of God was above the power of nature.

*Then sang Deborah and Barak
the son of Abinoam on that day, saying,
Praise ye the Lord for the avenging of
Israel, when the people willingly offered
themselves. Hear, O ye kings; give ear,
O ye princes; I, even I, will sing unto the
Lord; I will sing praise to the Lord God
of Israel. Lord, when thou wentest out of
Seir, when thou marchedst out of the field
of Edom, the earth trembled, and the
heavens dropped, the clouds also dropped
water. The mountains melted from before
the Lord, even that Sinai from before
the Lord God of Israel.*

JUDGES 5:1–5

A few minutes after my fourth child was born, he lay in my arms wrapped in a little blanket. I was sitting in a rocking chair by the side of the bed where my wife lay resting. The three of us were alone there. We had been in the hospital for only seventeen minutes. Imagine how quickly he was born.

Everything was warm—my wife, my baby, my tears. I began to sing. I sang hymns of love, I prayed in thanksgiving, and I praised God. My prayers were no bigger than my baby, soft like his blanket. There was nothing else to do. Nothing. There was no past, no future, no one but the four of us—the woman, the man, the baby boy, and their God.

You praise God because there is nothing else to say. As in the days of Deborah's Song, everything is over, it is done. All is well. Certainly there is more to come, but at present there is a great victory for Israel or, in my case, a baby boy. Praise is no effort, it is unscheduled; it is an honest response to God's work.

The Song of Deborah is one of the oldest writings of the Old Testament. Dating from 1125 B.C., it was written when the Israelites defeated the Canaanites at Taanach. It chants:

> Awake, awake, Deborah:
> Awake, awake, utter a song:
> Arise, Barak, and lead thy captivity captive,
> thou son of Abinoam (Judges 5:12).

Somebody had to wake up. For twenty years the Canaanites had oppressed Israel in their own land. The people suffered; spiritual life ebbed; there was not a man in Israel with courage enough to stand with God against this enemy. The people were silent, unbelieving. Then a woman's voice was heard.

Deborah, sitting under a palm tree between Ramah and Bethel, judged Israel (4:4). This means that she was a teacher and leader wisely adjudicating disputes. Maybe it was under that palm tree that she heard the voice of God: "Awake, Deborah. Arise, Barak. Lead thy captivity captive!" This they did, defeating the Canaanites.

Then, like me when my desire had come, they sang praises to God "and the land had rest forty years" (5:31).

DAY TWENTY-TWO

*Then Manoah intreated the Lord,
and said, O my Lord, let the man of God
which thou didst send come again unto us,
and teach us what we shall do unto
the child that shall be born.
And God hearkened to the voice of
Manoah; and the angel of God came again
unto the woman as she sat in the field.*

JUDGES 13:8–9

I spent summers during my college years working as a guide in the lakes of northern Minnesota and southern Ontario. On my first trip alone as a guide, I led a dozen people carrying four canoes into Canada. On our second morning we broke camp on Basswood, a large lake that straddles the border, and off we went.

I was paddling confidently in the lead canoe, looking for a certain landmark near the portage into smaller, more northerly lakes. After a long time, I noticed that the pattern of the shoreline looked familiar. We'd passed that way a short time before. Then it dawned on me that I didn't know where I was on that big lake. The others had been following me all morning as I circled a large island several times. I felt sick.

We put ashore to eat lunch, and I swallowed my pride, confessing to one or two of my companions. Together we consulted the map and compass and found our way out of Basswood. This experience taught me at least two things: when traveling, trust the map and ask directions.

That's why I like Manoah's prayer.

One day Manoah's wife told him that an awe-inspiring man who looked like an angel had come to her saying she was to have a child. She neglected to ask this man his name or where he came from. Moreover, the awe-inspiring man told her this baby boy would grow up "to deliver Israel out of the hand of the Philistines" (Judges 13:5). Manoah was quite confused. So he confessed that, like me on Basswood Lake, he had no idea how to go on. He asked God for directions. "Teach us what we are to do concerning the boy who will be born" (Judges 13:8 NRSV). This simple prayer opened the door for Manoah and his wife to enter into a marvelous experience with this angel of the Lord.

Anyone can be confused about life. Doesn't it happen to most people at least once? I like Manoah because he had no idea what was going on and admitted it when he prayed, "Teach us what we are to do" (v. 8 NRSV). I want to pray like him.

*And she was in bitterness of soul,
and prayed unto the Lord, and wept sore.
And she vowed a vow, and said,
O Lord of hosts, if thou wilt indeed look
on the affliction of thine handmaid,
and remember me, and not forget thine
handmaid, but wilt give unto thine
handmaid a man child, then I will give
him unto the Lord all the days of his life,
and there shall no razor come upon his
head. And it came to pass, as she continued
praying before the Lord, that Eli marked
her mouth. Now Hannah, she spake
in her heart; only her lips moved,
but her voice was not heard: therefore
Eli thought she had been drunken.*

1 SAMUEL 1:10–13

How does God answer prayer? Here is how it happened to Hannah. She was one of two wives of Elkanah. The other wife, Peninnah, had several children and constantly tormented Hannah because of her childlessness. Even when her husband reassured her that he loved her best, Hannah "wept and would not eat" (1 Samuel 1:7 NRSV). During an annual visit to the tabernacle in Shiloh, Hannah was so distressed that she approached the tabernacle in tears, praying for a son and promising to dedicate him to God's service. The high priest, Eli, saw her apparently talking to herself and thought her unusual behavior was caused by drunkenness. He scolded her for her unseemly actions.

Hannah replied, "No, my lord, I am a woman of a sorrowful spirit: I have drunken neither wine nor strong drink, but have poured out my soul before the Lord. . . . Then Eli answered and said, Go in peace: and the God of Israel grant thee thy petition that thou hast asked of him. And she said, Let thine handmaid find grace in thy sight. So the woman went her way, and did eat, and her countenance was no more sad" (1 Samuel 1: 15, 17–18).

The story goes on to tell how Hannah conceived and gave birth to Samuel and brought him back to Shiloh when he was weaned. Fulfilling her vow, she gave him over to the service of God in gratitude for the granting of her request.

In the patriarchal society of Hannah's day, both the responsibility of bearing a son and the burden of infertility fell unjustly on the woman. Despite her husband's love, Hannah was extremely distraught because of her infertility. Many women today share this same grief.

How did God answer Hannah's prayer for a child? After praying at Shiloh, she received reassurance from the high priest (v. 17). Prayer and encouragement caused Hannah to regain her spirits and resume eating. Her fertility was restored. Within a few months, Hannah conceived the son she had prayed for.

And the Lord came, and stood,
and called as at other times,
Samuel, Samuel.
Then Samuel answered,
Speak; for thy servant heareth.

1 SAMUEL 3:10

Samuel had no idea that God was calling to him. This young servant of Eli the high priest was only accustomed to answering the old man's nocturnal calls. Three times he heard his name, "Samuel, Samuel" (1 Samuel 3: 4, 6, 8) and thought it was Eli calling. Then God tried a fourth time, and thanks to some instruction from Eli (v. 9) the boy answered the divine call.

Not many biblical characters heard their

names when they were called by God. Earlier, God called, "Abraham, Abraham" (Genesis 22:11), and later another man heard the call, "Saul, Saul" (Acts 22:7). Abraham's answer seems casual: "Here I am" (Genesis 22:11). Perhaps this is because he was the friend of God (2 Chronicles 20:7; Isaiah 41:8; James 2:23). Saul, on the other hand, was God's enemy (Acts 22:8). He answered with fear and puzzlement, "Who are you?" This naive question admitted Saul to a crash course on the identity of God.

Though Samuel had Eli for a teacher, he "did not yet know the Lord, neither was the word of the Lord yet revealed unto him" (1 Samuel 3:7). Still he knew enough to say, "Speak; for thy servant heareth" (v. 10). Anyone who wishes to know the Lord and know the word of the Lord must possess this prayer: "Speak; for thy servant heareth." When we come to read the word of God or listen to its preaching, let's be so inclined: "Speak; for thy servant heareth." Like Habakkuk:

I will stand at my watchpost,
and station myself on the rampart;

I will keep watch to see what
he will say to me (Habakkuk 2:1 NRSV).

The fourth time Samuel heard his name from the mouth of God, he did not rise up but lay still and listened. Samuel's watchpost was his bed, tucked away somewhere in the Tabernacle. There God appeared—"The Lord came, and stood, and called"—yet the boy-prophet was quiet, with no tumult, no passion, composed and at rest. A believer with such a spirit prays, "Speak; for thy servant heareth."

*Now make us a king to judge us
like all the nations.
But the thing displeased Samuel,
when they said, Give us a king to judge us.
And Samuel prayed unto the Lord.
And the Lord said unto Samuel,
Hearken unto the voice of the people in all
that they say unto thee: for they have not
rejected thee, but they have rejected me,
that I should not reign over them.*

1 SAMUEL 8:5–7

Israel already had a king. Their problem was
that they couldn't see him. All they could see
was rumpled old Samuel, God's representa-
tive. It didn't matter that he was in direct

85

communication with the heavenly court and conversant in the visions of the Almighty. Samuel looked lowly in the eyes of the men who judged by outward appearance—Israel's elders. Who wants a poor solitary prophet in a mantle? A king in a purple robe with guards and officers of state would look great.

They should have been cheering like this: "For what nation is there so great, who hath God so nigh unto them, as the Lord our God is in all things that we call upon him for?" (Deuteronomy 4:7). Instead, they were begging, "Give us a king." If this pathetic appeal were granted, Israel would resemble the nations that had no such God. So Samuel prayed and God reminded him that this is "[what] they have done since the day that I brought them up out of Egypt" (1 Samuel 8:8).

A millennium later, Israel still didn't know how good they had it. Then their heavenly king came to them personally and lived among them. But they were still judging by outward appearance and taking the way of the world. He looked like a Nazarene carpenter, he made friends with sinners, he died a criminal. Later they were asked, "Which of the prophets did your ancestors not persecute? They killed those who foretold the coming of the Righteous One, and now you have become his betrayers and murderers" (Acts 7:52 NRSV).

That was the first century, and we are the church of the twenty-first century, blessed by God in Christ "with all spiritual blessings in heavenly places" (Ephesians 1:3). We all must remember that "these things happened to [Israel] to serve as an example, and they were written down to instruct us, on whom the ends of the ages have come. So if you think you are standing, watch out that you do not fall. . . . Therefore, my dear friends, flee from the worship of idols. I speak as to sensible people; judge for yourselves what I say" (1 Corinthians 10:11–12, 14–15 NRSV).

And now, O Lord God, thou art that God, and thy words be true, and thou hast promised this goodness unto thy servant: Therefore now let it please thee to bless the house of thy servant, that it may continue for ever before thee: for thou, O Lord God, hast spoken it: and with thy blessing let the house of thy servant be blessed for ever.

2 SAMUEL 7:28–29

My son comes to me about once a week asking for money. This is fine with me. Unless he has a summer job, I figure that my money is also his. I simply ask him what he's going to use the money for. I want to be sure that his purposes match mine. He usually uses the money to pay his cafeteria account at school, go to ball games, and go out with his friends. That's about it.

Prayers in the Bible are often like this. People ask God for that which he has already promised, and their prayers match God's purpose. David did this all the time. I invite you to read 2 Samuel 7:4–17—God's amazing blessing of David. Here is part of it: "I will be his father, and he shall be my son. . .my mercy shall not depart away from him. . .thine house and thy kingdom shall be established for ever before thee: thy throne shall be established for ever" (vv. 14–16).

Then David prays this right back to God, twice: "Therefore now let it please thee to bless the house of thy servant, that it may continue for ever before thee. . .and with thy blessing let the house of thy servant be blessed for ever" (v. 29). This is the kind of prayer that is answered.

It is no different for modern believers. If you want to be blessed, pray for what God already intends to give you. Ephesians 1 includes a comprehensive list of blessings that are according to God's purpose. It begins, "Blessed be the God and Father of our Lord Jesus Christ, who hath blessed us with all spiritual blessings in heavenly places in Christ" (v. 3). There follows a long list of blessings. Pray and praise about these things:

- God chose you in Christ before the world was made (v. 4).
- The reason for this is that you would be holy and blameless in love (v. 4).
- You are destined to be adopted as God's children through Jesus Christ (v. 5).
- God has bestowed on you his glorious grace in the beloved Son (v. 6).
- You have redemption through Jesus' blood (v. 7).
- You also have forgiveness of your sins (v. 7).
- God has made known to you the mystery of his will (v. 9).
- God wants you to live for the praise of his glory (v. 12).
- You are marked with the seal of the promised Holy Spirit (v. 13).
- The Holy Spirit is the guarantee of your future inheritance (v. 14).

These are richer blessings than David ever received.

*And the Lord struck the child that
Uriah's wife bare unto David,
and it was very sick. David therefore
besought God for the child;
and David fasted, and went in,
and lay all night upon the earth.
And the elders of his house arose, and went
to him, to raise him up from the earth:
but he would not, neither did he eat bread
with them. . . . Then David arose from the
earth, and washed, and anointed himself,
and changed his apparel, and came into
the house of the Lord, and worshipped:
then he came to his own house; and when
he required, they set bread before him,
and he did eat.*

2 SAMUEL 12:15–17, 20

Isn't the Bible wonderful in the way it uses language? I love these words, so strong and clear: "David fasted, and went in, and lay all night upon the earth." I can almost see him praying there for the desperately ill newborn child.

What do you think David was saying to God? Was he asking, "Why is this happening to me?" Not a chance. David knew full well why his baby was afflicted. He had lusted after Bathsheba, sent her husband Uriah to die in battle, and had taken her to his bed where she conceived the child that now lay dying. You must read the complete story in 2 Samuel 11:1–12:25.

When the prophet Nathan confronted David with his sin, David cried: "I have sinned against the Lord!" (12:13). Then Nathan told him that the child would die. Still, for seven days it was within the reach of prayer.

Lust, deceit, murder, adultery—such sins were amplified by David's exalted position as the divinely anointed king of Israel and patriarch of an eternal lineage (7:16). David's repentance from these sins became the prayer of Psalm 51, called "the brightest gem in the whole book [of

Psalms] and contains instruction so large and doctrine so precious that the tongue of angels could not do justice to the full development" (Victorinus Strigelius, 1524–1560).

Don't you think that this prayer will suffice for your sins? Add the words of Psalm 51 to your prayers. It could change your life like it did David's, who "arose from the earth, and washed, and anointed himself, and changed his apparel, and came into the house of the Lord, and worshipped: then he came to his own house; and when he required, they set bread before him, and he did eat" (12:20).

*And Gad came that day to David,
and said unto him, Go up,
rear an altar unto the Lord in the
threshingfloor of Araunah the Jebusite. . . .
So David bought the threshingfloor
and the oxen for fifty shekels of silver.
And David built there an altar
unto the Lord, and offered burnt
offerings and peace offerings.
So the Lord was intreated for the land,
and the plague was stayed from Israel.*

2 Samuel 24:18, 24–25

"There is an outcropping of starkly bare, rough limestone rock in Jerusalem which for thirty centuries past has gripped the minds and hearts of sons of men as being the most sacred spot on earth, known to the Jews as the Temple Mount and to the Moslems as the Noble Sanctuary. Tradition and legend blend together where it is difficult to separate the two. . . . Few places in the world have been. . .as sacred as this city, this flattened mountain and this rock" (Solomon Steckoll, *The Temple Mount*).

And to think that this holy place was once the threshingfloor of a farmer named Araunah.

A threshingfloor was a level, windy place where grain was separated from chaff in a two-step process. First, the cut and dried stalks of grain were spread on the threshingfloor, and a threshing sledge was pulled over the stalks by oxen. The sledge was a simple wooden sled with stone or metal spikes on the bottom that would break the heads of grain from the stalks (Isaiah 41:15–16). Then the broken stalks were tossed into the air with a large fan-shaped pitchfork made of wood. The wind would blow the lighter chaff to the side, while the heavier grain would fall into a pile. The process of separating grain from chaff using the wind is called winnowing (Ruth 3:2).

The threshingfloor of Araunah (whom the Bible also calls Ornan) was located on Mount Moriah, the place where Abraham offered Isaac to God (Genesis 22:2); the place where Solomon built the Temple (2 Chronicles 3:1) at the center of Jerusalem. God called this "my holy mountain" where he would bring his people "and make them joyful in my house of prayer. . .for mine house shall be called an house of prayer for all people" (Isaiah 56:7).

So it can be said that prayer takes place on a threshingfloor where dry, useless chaff is separated from nourishing grain. Those who persistently give themselves to prayer will sooner or later experience such a spiritual separation in their heart. This is what Christ does: "His winnowing fork is in his hand, to clear his threshing floor and to gather the wheat into his granary; but the chaff he will burn with unquenchable fire" (Luke 3:17 NRSV).

Give therefore thy servant an understanding heart to judge thy people, that I may discern between good and bad: for who is able to judge this thy so great a people? And the speech pleased the Lord, that Solomon had asked this thing.

1 Kings 3:9–10

The apostle James may have had Solomon in mind when he advised, "If any of you lack wisdom, let him ask of God, that giveth to all men liberally." Amazingly, James guarantees God's answer: "and it shall be given him" (James 1:5). You may say that you lack wisdom all the time, but this is not true. In our day-to-day affairs we know what to do: We get to work on time, pay our bills, drive carefully, eat sensibly, and so on. These things occupy most of our days. Wisdom is needed in unusual circumstances. You may have some conflict with a fellow worker or strife at home. Someone may be seriously ill, requiring medical decisions. In conditions like these, pause and pray; don't act until God gives wisdom.

Solomon's prayer rises above even these things. He tells when wisdom is needed each and every time. "Give therefore thy servant an understanding heart to judge thy people," he prays, "for who is able to judge this thy so great a people?" When it comes to working with the church, those people who are redeemed by faith in Christ, there is never a time when wisdom is not needed. Cooking in the church kitchen or delivering a sermon, we are among God's "so great a people," and nobody but God has the wisdom for this. In these circumstances, everyone lacks wisdom and, when asked, God supplies it liberally.

The problem is, when working among the people of the church, we must put ourselves aside. Solomon did this. When he prayed for wisdom, God answered, "Because thou hast asked this thing, and hast not asked for thyself long life; neither hast asked riches for thyself, nor hast asked the life of thine enemies; but hast asked for thyself understanding to discern judgment; Behold, I have done according to thy words" (1 Kings 3:11, 12).

It "pleased the Lord, that Solomon had asked this thing" (v. 10). Solomon desired to serve God's honor more than to advance himself. He shows us that those who prefer spiritual blessings to earthly favors are accepted by God.

*And it came to pass at the time
of the offering of the evening sacrifice,
that Elijah the prophet came near,
and said, Lord God of Abraham, Isaac,
and of Israel, let it be known this day
that thou art God in Israel, and that I am
thy servant, and that I have done all these
things at thy word. Hear me, O Lord, hear
me, that this people may know that thou
art the Lord God, and that thou hast
turned their heart back again.*

1 KINGS 18:36–37

Israel had been swept away from God by the worship of Baal—the fertility god of Canaanite tribes. This deity was so popular that there were

450 priests of Baal among the people and but one prophet for the Lord—Elijah (1 Kings 18:22). He offered the above prayer during a contest to determine the genuine god (vv. 23–40).

An outstanding element of his prayer is the mentioning of the names Abraham, Isaac, and Israel (Jacob). These three were the patriarchs of Israel, the ones who first displayed faith in God. Elsewhere, the Scripture enshrines them: "By faith Abraham. . .went out, not knowing whither he went. . . . By faith Isaac blessed Jacob and Esau concerning things to come. . . . By faith Jacob, when he was a dying. . .worshipped, leaning upon the top of his staff (Hebrews 11:8, 20–21).

All around Elijah stood thousands of Israelites, all of them knowing how their ancestors believed in God. As children they were told the stories of Abraham, Isaac, and Jacob. Although the faith of their fathers and mothers from generations past had waned, Elijah fanned the embers of that faith by crying out, "Lord God of Abraham, Isaac, and of Israel!" Reminded of the indomitable trust of their ancestors, faith began to well up in the hearts of the gathered Israelites and added its strength to the prophet's confidence in the God of Israel. "Then the fire of the Lord fell, and consumed the burnt sacrifice, and the wood, and the stones, and the dust, and licked up the water that was in the trench" (1 Kings 18:38). This display caused those Israelites to again believe in the Lord (v. 39).

Throughout the Bible we are urged to remember our heritage in the faith. For Israel, it was Abraham, Isaac, Jacob, and others. For us, it is also New Testament saints such as Mary, Peter, Paul, Priscilla, and those who followed them through two millennia. I pray that the church's history will not be forgotten among the common believers. If this occurs, our faith will be weakened. I hope that the old hymns will prevail and be enjoyed among us—hymns like "Faith of Our Fathers" by Frederick Faber (1814–1863):

Faith of our fathers! living still
In spite of dungeon, fire and sword;
O how our hearts beat high with joy
Whene'er we hear that glorious word!
Faith of our fathers, holy faith,
We will be true to thee till death.

And Jabez called on the God of Israel,
saying, Oh that thou wouldest bless me
indeed, and enlarge my coast, and
that thine hand might be with me,
and that thou wouldest keep me from evil,
that it may not grieve me! And God
granted him that which he requested.

1 CHRONICLES 4:10

What I like about Jabez is that he was a nobody.
Even 1 Chronicles doesn't tell us who he was.
The main purpose of the early chapters of this
book is to record the genealogies of Israel so there
will be no disputes about the inheritance of the
good land. It drones on and on with lists of
names. Then, in chapter four, Jabez comes out of

nowhere. His name is not connected with any family. The book does not record the name of his father or mother or brothers. Who was this guy? No one knows.

The one thing that distinguished Jabez is that he prayed. If he had not done this, we would have never heard of him and the Bible would not say that "God granted him that which he requested." This was his inheritance. Let this be an encouragement to all of us who are nobodies. Pray! We can pray, and God will hear.

Isn't this a prime lesson of the Bible—to pray always (Luke 21:36), to pray without ceasing (1 Thessalonians 5:17)? The book of Acts, the story of the emerging church, records in nearly every chapter that someone was praying. Redemption was accomplished so that we could "enter into the holiest by the blood of Jesus, by a new and living way, which he hath consecrated for us" (Hebrews 10:19–20).

Remember the apostle John? In the end he was a has-been, an old man exiled to Patmos Island. The world was going on without him. Then he wrote, "I was in the Spirit on the Lord's day, and heard behind me a great voice, as of a trumpet" (Revelation 1:10). Certainly, he was praying the day he heard the voice that gave him the revelation of the coming of Christ, the end of time and the eternal city, New Jerusalem. From this prayerful old man came what is arguably the most powerful book ever written.

John was with Jesus when he told the parable of Luke 18:1–8 to teach us about our "need to pray always and not to lose heart" (v. 1 NRSV). Let us daily ask ourselves the question that ends this parable: "When the Son of Man comes, will he find faith on earth?" (v. 8 NRSV). Will he find you praying?

O our God, wilt thou not judge them?
for we have no might against this great
company that cometh against us;
neither know we what to do:
but our eyes are upon thee.

2 CHRONICLES 20:12

If dogs could talk they would say, "Smelling is believing," because they navigate through this world using their nose. We humans depend on our eyesight much more than our other senses, so we say, "Seeing is believing." Here in 2 Chronicles believing Jehoshaphat says, "Our eyes are upon thee."

Jerusalem was faced with "a great multitude" of hostile Moabites, Ammonites, and Meunites.

This army was hastening toward the city for battle (vv. 1–2 NRSV). Jehoshaphat was powerless against this onslaught and made an articulate prayer to God (vv. 5–12). In the end he tells the Lord, "Our eyes are upon thee." Saying this, Jehoshaphat made God his leader. Soldiers in battle always keep their eyes on their leader. He is the one who knows the overall strategy, makes the decisions, and directs his troops to carry out the battle plan. If soldiers lose touch with their officers, their lives are in jeopardy and the battle lost.

The gospel of John says that God is spirit (4:24), undetectable with our four senses; still we must keep our eyes on God. This is possible because we believers have a set of eyes called the eyes of our heart: "I pray that the God of our Lord Jesus Christ, the Father of glory, may give you a spirit of wisdom and revelation as you come to know him, so that, with the eyes of your heart enlightened, you may know what is the hope to which he has called you. . . ." (Ephesians 1:17–18 NRSV).

The King James Version says, "the eyes of your understanding" (v.18), but the word translated, *understanding* is sometimes rendered as *heart*. Although our hearts were darkened before we believed (4:18 NRSV), now our hearts have eyes for God.

Jehoshaphat was at war and had to keep his eyes on his divine captain. But if we are not in the thick of spiritual warfare, why do we keep our eyes on God? Because of our love for God. In prayer, the eyes of our heart are opened to see the Lord. Continuing in prayer, our inner eyes become "like the fishpools in Heshbon, by the gate of Bathrabbim" (Song of Solomon 7:4)—wide open, looking up to God in love, reflecting the heavens.

*For a multitude of the people,
even many of Ephraim, and Manasseh,
Issachar, and Zebulun, had not cleansed
themselves. . . . But Hezekiah prayed for
them, saying, The good Lord pardon every
one that prepareth his heart to seek God,
the Lord God of his fathers, though he be
not cleansed according to the purification
of the sanctuary. And the Lord hearkened
to Hezekiah, and healed the people.*

2 CHRONICLES 30:18–20

What do you think makes you pure in God's
eyes?

In Hezekiah's day, the people of Israel hadn't
worshipped at the Temple in Jerusalem for many

years because they had divided themselves from Judah, so none of them had been ritually purified for all that time. Hezekiah invited Israel to come to Jerusalem in Judah for the Passover feast. There was no way this multitude could be made pure for the ceremony as the law required. So Hezekiah prayed for them, and God personally made them pure without the necessary ritual. We are purified by God alone, not by what we do.

The ancient Jews possessed detailed instructions from God about how to worship properly. They had all kinds of laws and rules and customs that controlled their behavior, especially in the yearly sacrifices and feasts. In this case, all those things were set aside, and thousands of people from the northern kingdom of Israel walked right in and enjoyed the Passover.

The ceremonial preparation at the Temple was probably lacking. The priests could not provide for the purification of all those people, so Hezekiah prayed for "every one that prepareth his heart to seek God." The fact is that no amount of ritual, church attendance, or participation can change a person without personal, private preparation in the inward parts. Though the former things are good and necessary, they are nothing without the latter. As David the king once prayed, "You desire truth in the inward being; therefore teach me wisdom in my secret heart. . .wash me, and I shall be whiter than snow" (Psalm 51:6–7 NRSV).

Truth in the inward being reveals that "the sacrifices of God are a broken spirit: a broken and a contrite heart, O God, thou wilt not despise" (v. 17). If you prepare your heart in prayer before you go to worship or serve the Lord, you'll notice that your inward being is more engaged in your worship. You will make heart-work of it.

DAY THIRTY-FOUR

*Then were assembled unto me
every one that trembled at the words
of the God of Israel,
because of the transgression of those
that had been carried away;
and I sat astonied until the evening
sacrifice. And at the evening sacrifice
I arose up from my heaviness;
and having rent my garment
and my mantle, I fell upon my knees,
and spread out my hands unto the Lord
my God, And said, O my God,
I am ashamed and blush to lift up my
face to thee, my God: for our iniquities
are increased over our head, and our
trespass is grown up unto the heavens.*

Ezra 9:4–6

We must beware of deceiving ourselves by denying or excusing our sins. Even Ezra struggled and was embarrassed to come to God in confession. Yes, it is hard to admit, even privately to God, "I did this or that sin. I love this or that thing more than I love you, my God." But the more we see our sins, the more we will treasure the love of God who sent his only begotten Son.

The Christian faith is the faith of sinners, of those who have sinned and in whom sin still dwells. That is why Jesus said, "I came not to call the righteous, but sinners to repentance" (Luke 5:32). This is why the Christian life is a life of continued repentance of sin. Not only so, it is a life of continual faith in Christ, thankfulness for his redemptive death, love to God who sent him, and joyful expectation of the glorious day of redemption, when the believers will be fully acquitted and sin abolished forever.

"If we say that we have no sin, we deceive ourselves, and the truth is not in us. If we confess our sins, he is faithful and just to forgive us our sins, and to cleanse us from all unrighteousness. If we say that we have not sinned, we make him a liar, and his word is not in us" (1 John 1:8–10).

The denial of sin flies in the face of the truth that says, "All have sinned, and come short of the glory of God" (Romans 3:23). If we say either that we have not sinned or do not still sin, the word of God is not in us.

The little biblical book that informs us of these uncomfortable truths is the first epistle of John, the book to turn to if you want to know about love, which is mentioned at least twenty-five times among 104 verses. The door of love swings open on the hinges of our confession and God's forgiveness.

Thou, even thou, art Lord alone;
thou hast made heaven, the heaven
of heavens, with all their host, the earth,
and all things that are therein, the seas,
and all that is therein, and thou
preservest them all; and
the host of heaven worshippeth thee.

NEHEMIAH 9:6

America was built by forward-looking people who did not dwell on the past. Instead, they remade the country again and again, creating a land that seems to be continually fresh. They were able to leave the old world for the new. They made New York, New Jersey, and New Hampshire, then moved on to new places on this continent. The migration lasted nearly two centuries, ending about a hundred years ago, when the frontier closed.

Although there is interest in the cultural, political, and natural history of this country, if there is a profit to be made, pity the old buildings, the old neighborhoods, or the old-growth forests, because Americans will tear them down to make something new.

But the way of the Bible is to remember the past and value it. The biblical prophets and poets often review history to bring Israel back to the way of God. Ezra's prayer in Nehemiah 9:6 begins a summary of Israel's history that runs until the end of the chapter. Read this story and see how it is a chronicle of failure. God's chosen people just could not get it right. But God remained steady. Ezra prayed, "But you are a God ready to forgive, gracious and merciful, slow to anger and abounding in steadfast love, and you did not forsake them" (v. 17 NRSV).

Why didn't God forsake them? Because he called them for the purpose of bringing the Savior into the world. Scripture explains: "Now the promises were made to Abraham and to his offspring. . .who is Christ" (Galatians 3:16 NRSV). As we know, when Jesus was born in Bethlehem, the Savior came.

Then God started a new work, enacting a new covenant through the resurrection of Jesus Christ. We are the church, the centerpiece of God's work in this age, but let's not forget history and the lesson that Israel teaches. We are no less apt to fail God. Nonetheless, God will complete his purpose with the church and Christ will return to the earth. "But of that day and that hour knoweth no man, no, not the angels which are in heaven, neither the Son, but the Father. Take ye heed, watch and pray: for ye know not when the time is" (Mark 13:32–33).

Then Job arose, and rent his mantle,
and shaved his head, and fell down upon
the ground, and worshipped, and said,
Naked came I out of my mother's womb,
and naked shall I return thither:
the Lord gave, and the Lord hath taken
away; blessed be the name of the Lord.
In all this Job sinned not,
nor charged God foolishly.

Job 1:20–22

Rereading the story of Job, I'm reminded of the verse that says, "For the love of money is a root of all kinds of evil" (1 Timothy 6:10 NRSV). Job was the richest man in the East. He was also blameless and upright; he feared God and turned away from evil. Was he a godly man because God had blessed him so richly? This is what Satan thought. "Put forth thine hand now," Satan said to God, "and touch all that he hath, and he will curse thee to thy face" (Job 1:11). If this had happened, all of Job's riches would have turned to evil.

Wealth had not made Job a foolish man. His actions proved the wisdom that "one's life does not consist in the abundance of possessions" (Luke 12:15 NRSV). Job displayed the content of his life when he did not passionately throw off all his clothes or tear out his hair. Rather, in conformity to his culture, he deliberately tore his outer cloak and shaved his head. Job kept his temper and maintained the possession of his soul in the midst of this tragedy.

Job did not feel that he was robbed or wounded or maimed. He was only naked, just as he was when he was born. He may as well have quoted Moses: "For dust thou art, and unto dust shalt thou return" (Genesis 3:19); or Solomon: "And the dust returns to the earth as it was, and the breath returns to God who gave it" (Ecclesiastes 12:7 NRSV); or Paul: "For we brought nothing into this world, and it is certain we can carry nothing out" (1 Timothy 6:7).

We do not hear Job say, "I am to blame for what happened to my children." Nor does he say, "The Lord gave and the Chaldeans have taken away" or "God made me rich, and the devil has made me poor." Instead he honored God as both the source and owner of all that he had: "The Lord gave, and the Lord hath taken away; blessed be the name of the Lord" (Job 1:21).

Job's is the voice of all people who are sanctified by faith. We have the assurance that, despite all losses, our souls "will not be found naked. . .so that what is mortal may be swallowed up by life" (2 Corinthians 5:3–4 NRSV).

Moreover the Lord answered Job,
and said, Shall he that contendeth
with the Almighty instruct him?
he that reproveth God, let him answer it.
Then Job answered the Lord,
and said, Behold, I am vile;
what shall I answer thee?
I will lay mine hand upon my mouth.
Once have I spoken; but I will not answer:
yea, twice; but I will proceed no further.

JOB 40:1–5

I wish I could print here all of God's words to Job in chapter 38, when "the Lord answered Job out of the whirlwind, and said, Who is this that darkeneth counsel by words without knowledge? Gird up now thy loins like a man; for I will demand of thee, and answer thou me. Where wast thou when I laid the foundations of the earth? declare, if thou hast understanding" (Job 38:1–4).

God asks question after question to expose Job's utter ignorance of the divine ways. "Hast thou entered into the springs of the sea? or hast thou walked in the search of the depth? Have the gates of death been opened unto thee? or hast thou seen the doors of the shadow of death? Hast thou perceived the breadth of the earth? declare if thou knowest it all" (38:16–18). This goes on and on, and Job is perfectly silenced.

These questions pummeled Job like the wind and earthquake that shook Elijah on Mount Horeb (1 Kings 19:11); they scorched Job like the fire that came when the Lord passed by Elijah (v. 12). As Job 40 opens, Job has given no answer. God spoke again, but this time not out of the whirlwind (38:1). I think this was a still small voice like that which spoke to Elijah (1 Kings 19:12–13). Job's heart was finally pierced by the inner voice of God, and he cried in repentance, "I am vile!"

Wind, earthquake, and fire can pass through our lives in the form of great happenings or personal troubles. We can be shaken by tragedy or awed by auspicious events. All can mercifully open our spiritual ears to hear the still small voice and lead to true repentance, causing believers to willingly say to God, "I lay my hand upon my mouth" and be silent and be taught.

Day Thirty-Eight

*Then Job answered the Lord,
and said, I know that thou canst
do every thing, and that no thought
can be withholden from thee.
Who is he that hideth counsel
without knowledge? therefore
have I uttered that I understood not;
things too wonderful for me,
which I knew not.
Hear, I beseech thee, and I will speak:
I will demand of thee, and declare thou
unto me. I have heard of thee by the
hearing of the ear: but now mine eye
seeth thee. Wherefore I abhor myself,
and repent in dust and ashes.*

Job 42:1–6

In the midst of their long conversation, Job's friend Elihu taught him this prayer: "For has anyone said to God, 'I have endured punishment; I will not offend any more; teach me what I do not see'" (Job 34:31–32 NRSV). God answered this prayer and, through suffering and struggle, taught Job what he did not see. The book of Job tells of this man who has fallen into the hands of the living God (Hebrews 10:31) and discovered that "our God is a consuming fire" (Hebrews 12:29). This culminates in Job 42, when the anguished man prays, "I have heard of thee by the hearing of the ear: but now mine eye seeth thee. Wherefore I abhor myself, and repent in dust and ashes" (Job 42:5–6).

It is a mercy to be educated in the things of God by the instruction of the Bible and God's ministers. After all, "how shall they believe in him of whom they have not heard? and how shall they hear without a preacher?. . .So then faith cometh by hearing, and hearing by the word of God" (Romans 10:14, 17). Job was a great man, and righteous, but he knew God only by the hearing of the ear.

Such knowledge can truly change you. For

example, the apostle Paul gave the teaching of the book of Romans to cause "the renewing of your minds, so that you may discern what is the will of God—what is good and acceptable and perfect" (Romans 12:2 NRSV). Job's understanding of God made him a blameless, God-fearing man who was upright and turned away from evil (Job 1:1 NRSV).

It is through the hearing of the ear that God reveals his Son *to* us—faith comes by hearing. But the book of Job illustrates teaching by the rod of circumstances and the revelation of the engrafted word (James 1:21). This deeper teaching of God's Spirit reveals his Son *in* us (Galatians 1:16).

Job declared, "Now mine eye seeth thee." This way of teaching is so profound and effective that we "are changed into the same image from glory to glory, even as by the Spirit of the Lord" (2 Corinthians 3:18).

Day Thirty-Nine

*Also I heard the voice of the Lord, saying,
Whom shall I send, and who will go
for us? Then said I, Here am I; send me.
And he said, Go, and tell this people,
Hear ye indeed, but understand not;
and see ye indeed, but perceive not.*

ISAIAH 6:8–9

These verses record the historic moment when Isaiah responded to God's call. About 2,700 years ago, the year King Uzziah died (c. 742 B.C., 2 Chronicles 26:21), Isaiah was a twenty-five-year-old priest, born among the privileged classes in Judah and Jerusalem. He prophesied during the reigns of Jotham, Ahaz, and Hezekiah. Other prophets who were speaking

127

for God at that time were Amos, Hosea, and Micah. These facts of history are interesting to me because they show that an actual man, a young man, had this most intense experience of God.

Isaiah saw God upon the throne in the heavenly temple with seraphim above, crying out to one another, "Holy, holy, holy!" The sound shook the heavens. Young Isaiah was devastated by the sight and soon felt heat from the altar purifying his lips (Isaiah 6:1–7). Then, as if God could find no human willing to help, the divine voice said, "Whom shall I send, and who will go for us?"

It is unlikely that you and I will ever experience such a thing. We live in a different age under the new covenant of God's grace. In Isaiah's day, God spoke through various prophets. Today, God's speaking is through the Son, Jesus Christ (Hebrews 1:1–2). However, we are like Isaiah in this way: We have responded to God's call. This may not necessarily be a call to serve in foreign missions or translate the Bible or be a pastor. More likely, it is the call to be a mother, a wife, a husband with a commonplace job and duty to children.

At some point in our life, we willingly accepted our calling, not knowing what it would entail in sacrifice and suffering. In this way, we are also like Isaiah. Only after he said to God, "Here am I; send me" did he learn that the people would shut their ears and eyes to him; they would not comprehend or be healed (Isaiah 6:9–10). So it is with us in our ordinary lives. We had no idea how difficult our assignment would be, yet we go forward, even reaching out in prayer toward the prize of God's high calling in Christ Jesus (Philippians 4:19).

And in that day thou shalt say,
O Lord, I will praise thee: though thou
wast angry with me, thine anger is turned
away, and thou comfortedst me. Behold,
God is my salvation; I will trust,
and not be afraid: for the Lord Jehovah
is my strength and my song;
he also is become my salvation.
Therefore with joy shall ye draw
water out of the wells of salvation.

ISAIAH 12:1–3

There is a beautiful Bible story about a woman. She goes about her daily duties as usual, and as she is drawing water out of the town well, she encounters Jesus Christ. They talk together without the woman knowing he is the Savior until, at the right moment, Jesus says, "I that speak unto thee am he" (John 4:26). The revelation instantly changes this woman. Suddenly, she finds within herself "a well of water springing up into everlasting life" (v. 14), and she hurries to tell the townsfolk, "Come and see a man who told me everything I have ever done!" (v. 29 NRSV).

The time comes for each of us to learn who Jesus is. The above prayer from Isaiah 12 prophetically describes the moment this happens to Israel. It comes after an apocalyptic description of the coming of Christ with the kingdom: "On that day the root of Jesse shall stand as a signal to the peoples; the nations shall inquire of him, and his dwelling shall be glorious" (Isaiah 11:10 NRSV). They realize that God is not only God; God is salvation. The Lord is not just the source of strength; the Lord *is* their strength. They don't just sing about God; the Lord is their song. Then the wells of salvation open to them, and they joyously draw out the water of eternal life (12:1–3).

Today the resurrected Savior is standing amidst the world's crowd, crying out, "If any man thirst, let him come unto me, and drink. He that believeth on me, as the scripture hath said, out of his belly shall flow rivers of living water" (John 7:37–38). It doesn't seem to me that many people hear him above the din of mundane concerns, but the invitation to draw water from the wells of salvation will persist to the end, when "the Spirit and the bride say, Come. . .and let him that is athirst come. And whosoever will, let him take the water of life freely" (Revelation 22:17).

Each time a believer prays, he or she is kneeling on the banks of the river of water of life. Its waters flow clear as crystal out of the throne of God and of the Lamb (Revelation 22:1). "Behold, God is my salvation," we pray, drinking of the water of life. "I will trust, and not be afraid."

Yea, in the way of thy judgments,
O Lord, have we waited for thee;
the desire of our soul is to thy name,
and to the remembrance of thee.
With my soul have I desired thee in
the night; yea, with my spirit within me
will I seek thee early: for when thy
judgments are in the earth, the inhabitants
of the world will learn righteousness.

ISAIAH 26:8–9

The Bible tells a remarkable story about
serving the Lord. When Jesus and the disciples
were on their way to Jerusalem, they came to
Bethany where Martha gave them hospitality.
She busied herself in the kitchen preparing a

big meal for everyone. Meanwhile, her sister, Mary, sat with Jesus, listening to what he taught. Martha came to Jesus and said, "Lord, it's unfair that my sister just sits here while I do all the work. Tell her to come and help me." Jesus replied, "Dear Martha, there's really only one thing worth being concerned about, and Mary has discovered it. I won't take that away from her" (Luke 10:38–42, author's paraphrase).

Can you see Mary sitting with the Lord, hanging on every word he says? This is how Jesus wants us to serve him: to lovingly watch and listen to him. "Behold, as the eyes of servants look unto the hand of their masters, and as the eyes of a maiden unto the hand of her mistress; so our eyes wait upon the Lord our God, until that he have mercy upon us" (Psalm 123:2). The ultimate mercy will come on the day Christ returns, so we watch and wait for him. The desire of our soul is his name and the remembrance of him (Isaiah 26:8).

Christ himself instructed us how to watch and wait. On the night he was betrayed by Judas, Jesus took bread, gave thanks, broke it, and said, "This is my body, which is given for you. Do this in remembrance of me." Then he took a cup of wine and said, "This cup is the new covenant between you and God, confirmed by the shedding of my blood. As often as you drink it, remember me." When we eat the bread and drink of the cup, we remember the Lord, announcing his death, waiting until he comes again (see 1 Corinthians 11:23–26).

The world is riding the rough road of God's judgments. It seems to be going from bad to worse. But when we eat at the Lord's Table with its holy bread and cup, we find patience to wait for the Lord, love to desire his name, and wisdom to remember him until he returns.

*For our transgressions are multiplied
before thee, and our sins testify against us:
for our transgressions are with us;
and as for our iniquities, we know them;
In transgressing and lying against the
Lord, and departing away from our God,
speaking oppression and revolt, conceiving
and uttering from the heart words of
falsehood. . . And the Redeemer shall come
to Zion, and unto them that turn from
transgression in Jacob, saith the Lord.*

ISAIAH 59:12–13, 20

If Christians were to take biblical prayers as the
pattern for their own petitions to God, there
would be much more confession of sin among us.

Confession is a major topic of scriptural prayer. There must be a reason for this. Did those ancient seekers of God discover that confession of sin is a wonderful thing? I think so. One reason for this is the guarantee of forgiveness. As the apostle John wrote: "If we say that we have no sin, we deceive ourselves, and the truth is not in us. If we confess our sins, he is faithful and just to forgive us our sins, and to cleanse us from all unrighteousness" (1 John 1:8–9).

This potent promise reveals some important things that compelled the biblical seekers to confess. There is more than forgiveness in store for the repentant sinner—there is also cleansing. Unrighteousness is washed away. It is not just covered up, it is not simply forgotten—it is gone. This is nearly inconceivable to us because we have tremendous difficulty forgiving others. Even if we forgive, we cannot forget, much less expunge all trace of the offense. But God does this.

There is something even more marvelous in store for those who confess. Forgiveness is embodied in a person. John does not say, "If we confess, we will be forgiven." Rather he says that if we confess, a person responds—*"He is* faithful and just to forgive" (v. 9). Similarly, Isaiah tells Israel, "The Redeemer shall come to Zion" (Isaiah 59:20). The redeemer is God in Christ.

Divine forgiveness and cleansing are reasons enough to confess each and every transgression. Yet we are promised more: Christ, the faithful and righteous redeemer, will personally deliver forgiveness and cleansing to your soul. He is the object of your faith.

> To God be the glory, great things he
>   hath done,
> So loved he the world that he gave us
>   his Son,
> Who yielded his life an atonement for sin,
> And opened the life-gate that all may go in.
>
> O perfect redemption, the purchase of
>   blood,
> To ev'ry believer the promise of God;
> The vilest offender who truly believes,
> That moment from Jesus a pardon receives.

> Fanny Crosby (1820–1915)

*I have set watchmen upon thy walls,
O Jerusalem, which shall never hold their
peace day nor night: ye that make mention
of the Lord, keep not silence, and give him
no rest, till he establish, and till he make
Jerusalem a praise in the earth.*

ISAIAH 62:6–7

In the days of ancient Israel, the time between
sunset and sunrise was divided into three
watches: the beginning of the watches (Lamentations 2:19), the middle watch (Judges 7:19),
and the morning watch (Exodus 14:24;
1 Samuel 11:11). A city's watchmen relieved
each other at each of these periods. Their
purpose was to keep the city safe from its

enemies (2 Samuel 18:24–27; 2 Kings 9:17–20; Isaiah 21:5–9).

"I have set watchmen upon thy walls, O Jerusalem" (Isaiah 62:6) is a famous declaration of the existence of watchmen in the spiritual sense. These are not the actual watchmen who kept vigil over the physical city of Jerusalem; they are believers who pray until God makes Jerusalem gloriously renowned all over the earth. Isaiah says that this glory is like a marriage: "You shall be called My Delight Is in Her, and your land Married; for the Lord delights in you, and your land shall be married. For as a young man marries a young woman, so shall your builder marry you, and as the bridegroom rejoices over the bride, so shall your God rejoice over you (vv. 62:4–5 NRSV).

I would like to be a watchman like those in Isaiah 62:6–7. Wouldn't you? They are not required to shout cries of alarm. Instead, they are preparing for a wedding. They give God "no rest, till he establish, and till he make Jerusalem a praise in the earth." These watchmen are on the lookout for love, not war.

The church is like a bride to Christ. Their

relationship is one of eternal love: "Husbands, love your wives, even as Christ also loved the church, and gave himself for it" (Ephesians 5:25). Today there is need of watchmen to pray that Christ "might sanctify and cleanse [the church] with the washing of water by the word, that he might present it to himself a glorious church" (vv. 26–27). This will hasten the day when the voice of many waters and of mighty thunderings will say, "Let us be glad and rejoice, and give honour to him: for the marriage of the Lamb is come, and his wife hath made herself ready" (Revelation 19:6–7).

DAY FORTY-FOUR

*Oh that thou wouldest rend the heavens,
that thou wouldest come down,
that the mountains might flow down
at thy presence, as when the melting fire
burneth, the fire causeth the waters to boil,
to make thy name known to thine
adversaries, that the nations may tremble
at thy presence! When thou didst terrible
things which we looked not for, thou
camest down, the mountains flowed down
at thy presence. For since the beginning
of the world men have not heard, nor
perceived by the ear, neither hath the eye
seen, O God, beside thee, what he hath
prepared for him that waiteth for him.*

ISAIAH 64:1–4

Jesus Christ asks us the following piercing question about his second coming: "When the Son of Man comes, will he find faith on earth?" (Luke 18:8 NRSV). This question is asked in the context of a parable about persistent prayer. Jesus told the parable to encourage people to "pray always and not to lose heart" (v. 1). He hopes that such prayer will continue until the end.

In the midst of persistent prayer, believers become "able to comprehend with all saints what is the breadth, and length, and depth, and height; And to know the love of Christ, which passeth knowledge" (Ephesians 3:18–19). These are things that "eye hath not seen, nor ear heard, neither have entered into the heart of man, the things which God hath prepared for them that love him" (1 Corinthians 2:9).

True, "we know in part, and we prophesy in part. . . . We see through a glass, darkly (1 Corinthians 13:9, 12). Yet, thanks to our faith in the gospel, we have been included in "the fellowship of the mystery, which from the beginning of the world hath been hid in God" (Ephesians 3:9). The blessings of the gospel are a part of what God "hath prepared for him that waiteth for him" (Isaiah 64:4).

As Christians wait in prayer for the Lord's return, I hope our spiritual eyes and ears will be opened to know more of what God prepared for us. I hope that each heart will be prepared in love to exclaim, "The voice of my beloved! behold, he cometh leaping upon the mountains, skipping upon the hills" (Song of Solomon 2:8). I pray that every ear will hear the Lord say, "Rise up, my love, my fair one, and come away. For, lo, the winter is past, the rain is over and gone; the flowers appear on the earth; the time of the singing of birds is come, and the voice of the turtle is heard in our land" (vv. 10–12).

*Then said I, Ah, Lord God! behold,
I cannot speak: for I am a child.*

JEREMIAH 1:6

God told Jeremiah, "Before I formed you in the womb I knew you, and before you were born I consecrated you; I appointed you a prophet to the nations" (Jeremiah 1:5 NRSV). God designed and predestinated Jeremiah to an honorable line of work. The prophet-to-be modestly, though unsuccessfully, turned down the job.

None of us know exactly what God intends for us, but God knows. You may be like me and say, "Sure, God knew the great prophet Jeremiah from before the womb, but not me. I'm nobody." True, we're nobodies. But we're nobodies who love God, and "anyone who loves God is known by him" (1 Corinthians 8:3 NRSV). There's no getting around it: God has an assignment for you, and it is probably that which you have at hand right now.

You'd think that Jeremiah would have grabbed at the chance for such a great job, yet he was quite surprised to hear that he would be a prophet to the nations, and he claimed to be unqualified for it. "Ah, Lord God! Look, I can't speak to great men and multitudes like prophets do. I can't speak finely or fluently or word things like a message from God should be worded. I can't speak with any authority. I'm a child."

It is a good idea to be both willing and modest, if possible, when we have any service to do for God. Elihu is a good example of this. Note what he regarded as his sufficiency: "I am young, and ye are very old; wherefore I was afraid, and durst not shew you mine opinion. I said, Days should speak, and multitude of years should teach wisdom. But there is a spirit in man: and the inspiration of the Almighty giveth them understanding" (Job 32:6–8).

Yes, there is a spirit in each one of us

(1 Thessalonians 5:23). It is through our spirit that the inspiration of the Almighty gives us understanding. It is good to open your spirit to God by praying, "Lord, I am a child." But follow with this phrase: "And you are my Father; you are my sufficiency for every task."

Day Forty-Six

*O Lord, I know that the way of man is
not in himself: it is not in man that
walketh to direct his steps.
O Lord, correct me, but with judgment;
not in thine anger,
lest thou bring me to nothing.*

Jeremiah 10:23–24

Somewhere in the bottom of a box, I have a copy
of the front section of the *New York Times* with a
headline announcing the end of Soviet Com-
munism. It was as if a portion of the world had
been frozen in ice and was suddenly thawed. This
was a major historic event, so I kept the news-
paper from that day.

Since then, the world has been in a state

of flux as it hasn't been since World War II. National boundaries have changed, and whole new nations have emerged. Though the Soviet Union was terrible and dangerous in many ways, the world we inhabited with it was a familiar place. Now terror and danger come from other places, some of them with unheard-of names, and there is unease among us.

Jeremiah says "the way of man is not in himself" (10:23). That is, human beings do not control their existence. Another prophet explained it this way: "From one ancestor [God] made all nations to inhabit the whole earth, and he allotted the times of their existence and the boundaries of the places where they would live" (Acts 17:26 NRSV).

Like us, Jeremiah faced a changing world, as did all the inhabitants of Judah and Jerusalem. "Hear, a noise!" he proclaimed. "Listen, it is coming—a great commotion from the land of the north to make the cities of Judah a desolation, a lair of jackals" (Jeremiah 10:22 NRSV). Jerusalem was facing an invasion of the Chaldeans who would soon destroy the city and carry everyone away captive.

While reading the prayer from Jeremiah 10: 23–24, do you notice that Jeremiah didn't ask God to change the world? Instead, he asked God to correct his personal life. This is all he had available. It is all he could offer to God. Such correction is frightening, so Jeremiah asked, "Correct me, but with judgment." He wants God's correction in measure, with moderation, and in wisdom. We can't ask God to never correct us, but, like Jeremiah, we can ask that we would never be corrected through divine anger.

This prayer of Jeremiah teaches us that if we have the courage to ask for God's correction, the world will remain as it is, while our way of living in the world is changed.

We acknowledge, O Lord, our wickedness,
and the iniquity of our fathers:
for we have sinned against thee.
Do not abhor us, for thy name's sake,
do not disgrace the throne of thy glory:
remember, break not thy covenant with us.
Are there any among the vanities of
the Gentiles that can cause rain?
or can the heavens give showers?
art not thou he, O Lord our God?
therefore we will wait upon thee:
for thou hast made all these things.

JEREMIAH 14:20–22

Remember the story of the paralyzed man who was lowered through a roof to be healed by Jesus?

151

The story is told in Luke 5:18–26. At first Jesus didn't heal that man physically. This didn't seem to occur to him. Instead the Savior said, "Man, thy sins are forgiven thee" (v. 20). He first remedied the cause of the man's sickness, and only later did he remove the paralysis itself.

The prayer of Jeremiah 14:19–22 emerges from the prophet's desire for the spiritual healing of his nation. "Hast thou utterly rejected Judah?" he asked God. "Hath thy soul loathed Zion? why hast thou smitten us, and there is no healing for us? we looked for peace, and there is no good; and for the time of healing, and behold trouble!" (Jeremiah 14:19). The prophet eloquently confessed the sins of the people because he knew that their sin had brought trouble to them. Sin does this—it causes suffering and pain.

Jeremiah's confession is a pattern for our own. He expresses utter helplessness; he makes no vow or promise but throws himself in utter dependence on God. The prayer is strengthened only by the value of God's name and throne and covenant. Perhaps because he felt the burning of the people's sin, Jeremiah evokes images of refreshing rain, which would extinguish that fire. None of the vanities of the Gentiles—the world's comforts—can supply such relief.

Did you ever wonder, "What's wrong with me?" The true answer—sin—is the same for everyone. Only you and God know the details. Jeremiah knew the details of sin and, seeking forgiveness, threw himself upon all that God is. This is the way of confession and forgiveness. William Sleeper (1819–1904) wrote a beautiful hymn about this. Here are two of its verses:

Out of my bondage, sorrow, and night,
    Jesus, I come, Jesus, I come;
Into Thy freedom, gladness, and light,
    Jesus, I come to Thee;
Out of my sickness, into Thy health,
Out of my want and into Thy wealth,
Out of my sin and into Thyself,
    Jesus, I come to Thee.

Out of my shameful failure and loss,
    Jesus, I come, Jesus, I come;
Into the glorious gain of Thy cross,
    Jesus, I come to Thee;

Out of earth's sorrows into Thy balm,
Out of life's storms and into Thy calm,
Out of distress to jubilant psalm,
    Jesus, I come to Thee.

DAY FORTY-EIGHT

*Thy words were found,
and I did eat them; and thy word
was unto me the joy and rejoicing
of mine heart: for I am called by thy name,
O Lord God of hosts.*

JEREMIAH 15:16

I once leafed through a book catalog and marveled at the number of multi-volume Bible commentaries that it offered. There must have been dozens of them, each composed of five or ten volumes or more. They were written by all kinds of people. Each author spent years of his life studying the Bible, organizing all he learned, and writing it down for others. I wondered who reads these works and who receives help from them.

I have never worked on such books, but I have written, edited, and contributed to numerous books for Christian readers—Bibles, Bible storybooks, books of prayers and poems and devotional readings. I'd like to tell you a secret: The person who gets the most out of a book about the Bible is the author of that book.

The reason this is true is given by Jeremiah: "Thy words were found, and I did eat them." The author labors in the pages of the Bible with prayer and study until the words printed there come alive. Then he declares to God, "Thy words were found" *by me*, and I didn't just taste them, I ate them! They were food to a hungry man. I savored your words. Then I chewed and digested them. They nourished me and have become a part of me. Thy word is "unto me the joy and rejoicing of my heart."

My brother-in-law knows exactly when and where to collect wild berries, nuts, mushrooms, and other edibles. He can walk through the Oregon woods and come out well fed. If I were to walk through the same bunch of trees, I would find nothing to eat, but he has spent untold hours in the forest and easily finds food there.

I encourage you to go into the Bible, spend time there, and, like brother-in-law in the forest, find food. Do you have a Bible that doesn't have footnotes or study helps? Use that Bible and a concordance. That's all you need. Pray and consider only one verse. Look up its cross-references. Ask the Lord to make it live for you. Compare different translations. Pray for its meaning. In other words, find it and eat it. God deeply desires to hear you say, "Thy words were found, and I did eat them; and thy word was unto me the joy and rejoicing of mine heart."

Day Forty-Nine

*A glorious high throne from the beginning
is the place of our sanctuary.
O Lord, the hope of Israel,
all that forsake thee shall be ashamed,
and they that depart from me
shall be written in the earth,
because they have forsaken the Lord,
the fountain of living waters.
Heal me, O Lord, and I shall be healed;
save me, and I shall be saved:
for thou art my praise.*

Jeremiah 17:12–14

One sunny spring day when I was young, I was driving my car down the street feeling especially self-righteous. I didn't know I was basking in self-righteousness until I glanced at a young man walking down the sidewalk. That man's appearance caused a mean, judgmental thought to spontaneously leap into my mind. Almost simultaneously, a realization flashed before me: "You are no better than he." That was God's mercy. I've thought of myself and others differently from that day to this.

Jeremiah was surrounded by people who were forsaking God. He said they would soon be ashamed and their names written in the earth. They will be blown away like words written in the dust. They belong to the earth and are numbered among earthly people who lay up their treasure on earth; their names are not written in heaven (Hebrews 12:23). These are strong words—stronger than any judgment I could apportion in the days of my self-righteousness.

The difference between Jeremiah's thoughts and mine is seen in the last sentence of the prophet's prayer (Jeremiah 17:14). He prays to God for healing mercy for himself. It is as if he realizes, "If the case of those that depart from God is so miserable, I want to always draw near to God. So, Lord, heal me and save me from being carried away by the strength of the stream that forsakes you." In contrast, I had the mind of a Pharisee, thinking that I deserved my place in God's good graces. I knew that I could not lose my salvation, but I had somehow convinced myself that I deserved it and possessed enough strength in myself to remain with God.

Jeremiah didn't assume that he had the knack to remain in the flow of the fountain of living waters. "Heal me, O Lord, and then I shall be healed," he prayed. Jeremiah's cure would come only if it came from God—a thorough cure, not a Band-Aid. "Save me, and then I shall be saved." When God is our salvation, we are safe from forsaking the Lord's flowing fountain.

*It is of the Lord's mercies that we are not
consumed, because his compassions fail not.
They are new every morning: great is
thy faithfulness. The Lord is my portion,
saith my soul; therefore will I hope in him.
The Lord is good unto them that wait
for him, to the soul that seeketh him.
It is good that a man should both hope and
quietly wait for the salvation of the Lord.*

LAMENTATIONS 3:22–26

The book of Lamentations tells the story of the
destruction of Jerusalem in 586 B.C. According to
tradition, after the razing of Jerusalem by
Nebuchadnezzar, Jeremiah retreated to a cavern
outside the Damascus gate. There he wrote his

book. Tour guides still point out this "grotto of Jeremiah" in the face of a rocky hill on the western side of the city. Though the grotto story is doubtful, scholars agree that this series of five poems probably originated with the prophet. The spirit, tone, language, and subject matter of Lamentations match Jeremiah's style.

One poem comprises each chapter of the book. Each is well worth reading. In chapter 1, the prophet tells of the many miseries of the once-beautiful city that now sits sorely weeping, a solitary widow. In chapter 2, these miseries are seen in connection with the national sins that caused them. Chapter 3 speaks of hope for the people of God. Their chastisement will be for their good, and a better day will dawn for them. Chapter 4 laments the ruin and desolation of Jerusalem and her temple and lays the blame for this upon the city's sinful people. Chapter 5 is a prayer that Zion's reproach may be taken away in the repentance and recovery of her people.

It is good to consider Lamentations. These things happened and were written down to serve as an example to us (1 Corinthians 10:11), although Jerusalem's sufferings seem unbearable.

"He hath hedged me about, that I cannot get out: he hath made my chain heavy. Also when I cry and shout, he shutteth out my prayer. He hath inclosed my ways with hewn stone, he hath made my paths crooked" (Lamentations 3:7–9).

We all have our problems and our private sins, but do they compare with the problems that came upon the people of Jerusalem? Probably not, because God's promise to us is that "no testing has overtaken you that is not common to everyone. God is faithful, and he will not let you be tested beyond your strength" (1 Corinthians 10:13 NRSV). In other words, as Jeremiah prayed, "It is of the Lord's mercies that we are not consumed, because his compassions fail not" (Lamentations 3:22).

I called upon thy name,
O Lord, out of the low dungeon.
Thou hast heard my voice: hide not
thine ear at my breathing, at my cry.
Thou drewest near in the day that I called
upon thee: thou saidst, Fear not. O Lord,
thou hast pleaded the causes of my soul;
thou hast redeemed my life.

LAMENTATIONS 3:55–58

In the autumn of 1972, I was living in Santa Cruz, California. Intense dissatisfaction and loneliness had invaded my life. Regular meditation practice lessened my anxiety, and nearly every day I prayed to God. Somehow I had come to understand that a solution to the puzzle of my life would come from the divine source, but I did not know the way to God in Christ.

One day, a friend asked me to spend a few nights at her house. A prowler had been working the neighborhood, and she and her sisters and mother thought my presence would add some security to their home. One night I was there trying to go to sleep, but my mind would not allow it. I was thinking about my life—its past, present, and future. My mind raced wildly up and down among events and people and fears and hopes. I could not stop it. My eyes were wide open, and the room was very dark. There was no light inside or out. I was in a familiar dungeon of depression and fear.

I called on your name, O Lord, out of the low dungeon. "O Lord Jesus," I whispered. "O Lord Jesus."

You have heard my voice: do not hide your ear at my breathing, at my cry. Immediately light came into me, and the room itself seemed to ignite for an instant, though there was no physical illumination. Then I sensed love within me, divine love. *You came near when I called on you; you said, "Do not fear."*

I had no knowledge of the Bible. I did not know until that moment that Jesus Christ lives in resurrection or that he could make his home in my heart. I arose from bed, got dressed, and went out into the house and told whoever was there, "Christ is real. Christ is real!"

O Lord, you have pleaded the causes of my soul; you have redeemed my life.

Day Fifty-Two

*Then was the secret revealed unto
Daniel in a night vision.
Then Daniel blessed the God of heaven. . .
and said, Blessed be the name of God
for ever and ever: for wisdom and might
are his. . .he giveth wisdom unto the wise,
and knowledge to them that know
understanding: He revealeth the deep and
secret things: he knoweth what is in the
darkness, and the light dwelleth with him.*

Daniel 2:19–22

At three crucial moments in American history
great men have ascended to the presidency.
George Washington ushered in democracy.
Abraham Lincoln preserved the Union. Franklin

Roosevelt shepherded the country through the Great Depression. When history required, the right man was available to do a difficult job. As Daniel says, "[God] changeth the times and the seasons: he removeth kings, and setteth up kings."

Why does God do this? Because it suits the divine purpose. The work of God to fulfill this purpose is hard to pinpoint in our day-to-day lives or even in current world events, but it is clear in the biblical record.

After the destruction of Jerusalem and the removal of the people to Babylon, the focus of God's plan shifted to Chaldea and centered on the gifted man Daniel. The record tells that Daniel was about to be killed unless someone could interpret the king's dream (Daniel 2:12–15). This could not happen, despite the power of King Nebuchadnezzar or the impossibility of the situation. Daniel was crucial to God at that moment, so he was given the interpretation of the dream. This not only saved Daniel's life, it also supplied us with a revelation of world history. The image in Nebuchadnezzar's dream (vv. 31–45) represents all the kingdoms of the world relevant to God's purpose until the coming of the Kingdom of God.

When Daniel was given the dream's interpretation, he immediately offered the prayer of praise in verses 19–23. Daniel's prayer shows that he understood why God made this dream known. It was not to make Daniel a great man or to save the lives of the Chaldean astrologers and magicians. It was not done for Nebuchadnezzar or Chaldea or even the captive Jews. This all happened for God's benefit—"Wisdom and might," declared Daniel, "are his."

The familiar stories in the book of Daniel are marvelous. I began hearing them when I was just a boy. What I wasn't taught is that the captive Jews eventually returned to the promised land and rebuilt the Temple and the city of Jerusalem. I now find it interesting that Daniel is not numbered among those who returned. The miraculous events of his life advanced the purpose of God, who "giveth wisdom unto the wise, and knowledge to them that know understanding." Then God moved on and singled out others, such as Ezra and Nehemiah, to meet the needs of the eternal plan.

O Israel, return unto the Lord thy God;
for thou hast fallen by thine iniquity.
Take with you words,
and turn to the Lord: say unto him,
Take away all iniquity, and receive
us graciously: so will we render the calves
of our lips. Asshur shall not save us;
we will not ride upon horses: neither will
we say any more to the work of our hands,
Ye are our gods: for in thee the
fatherless findeth mercy.

HOSEA 14:1–3

"What shall I render unto the Lord for all his benefits toward me?" (Psalm 116:12). The psalmist asks a very good question, don't you think?

God has been so generous; what should we give in return? Ezra pondered this, too. "Our God has not forsaken us in our slavery, but has extended to us his steadfast love before the kings of Persia, to give us new life to set up the house of our God, to repair its ruins, and to give us a wall in Judea and Jerusalem. And now, our God, what shall we say after this?" (Ezra 9:9–10 NRSV).

Hosea gives the answer: "Take words with you and return to the Lord" (Hosea 14:2 NRSV). In Hosea's day, Israel had stumbled in sin, and so the prophet told them to bring not offerings, but words of repentant prayers. It was much easier for them to sacrificially slaughter a calf than to honestly confess, "Assyria shall not save us; we will not ride upon horses; we will say no more, 'Our God,' to the work of our hands" (Hosea 14:3 NRSV). God didn't want them to sacrifice actual calves. Instead, they were to offer the calves of their lips.

For us, the sacrifice is already offered. "Jesus also suffered outside the city gate in order to sanctify the people by his own blood" (Hebrews 13:12 NRSV). This is why there is no physical offering we can bring to God. The priceless offering of Jesus Christ was given for us long ago. Now we are only asked to do this: "Let us then go to him outside the camp and bear the abuse he endured. For here we have no lasting city, but we are looking for the city that is to come. Through him, then, let us continually offer a sacrifice of praise to God, that is, the fruit of lips that confess his name" (vv. 13–15).

"What shall I render unto the Lord for all his benefits toward me?" asks the psalmist. "I will take the cup of salvation, and call upon the name of the Lord. I will pay my vows unto the Lord now in the presence of all his people" (Psalm 116:12–14).

*Then Jonah prayed unto the Lord his
God out of the fish's belly. . . . The waters
compassed me about, even to the soul:
the depth closed me round about,
the weeds were wrapped about my head.
I went down to the bottoms of the
mountains; the earth with her bars was
about me for ever: yet hast thou brought up
my life from corruption, O Lord my God.*

JONAH 2:1, 5–6

In this book we've frequently discussed what
people pray about. Now we come to Jonah. His
experience brings up the topic of where people
pray. If "Jonah prayed unto the Lord his God out
of the fish's belly," then there is no wrong place

for prayer. This is especially true since the apostle Paul desired "that men pray every where, lifting up holy hands" (1 Timothy 2:8).

Ideally, God's temple in Jerusalem was to be a "house of prayer for all people" (Isaiah 56:7). Even if it had worked out that way, it would have been only one place on earth where people could legitimately pray with the pre-scribed animal sacrifices. But God had greater plans. Malachi sheds light on them: "For from the rising of the sun even unto the going down of the same my name shall be great among the Gentiles; and in every place incense shall be offered unto my name, and a pure offering" (Malachi 1:11).

Instead of being worshipped and served among the Jews only, a small people in a corner of the world, God wanted to be served and worshipped in all places. This makes sense. So God prepared a sacrifice by which "we are sanctified through the offering of the body of Jesus Christ once for all" (Hebrews 10:10). Now the heavens are equally accessible from every part of the earth. Praise the Lord!

Religions of all kinds characterize certain

places as more sacred than others, but unlike religions, God is not exclusive and is not limited to physical places. Jesus established this fact long ago when he spoke to a woman as he sat by a well:

> The woman saith unto him. . .Our fathers worshipped in this mountain; and ye say, that in Jerusalem is the place where men ought to worship. Jesus saith unto her, Woman, believe me, the hour cometh, when ye shall neither in this mountain, nor yet at Jerusalem, worship the Father. . . . But the hour cometh, and now is, when the true worshippers shall worship the Father in spirit and in truth: for the Father seeketh such to worship him. God is a Spirit: and they that worship him must worship him in spirit and in truth (John 4:19–21, 23–24).

Although the fig tree shall not blossom,
neither shall fruit be in the vines;
the labor of the olive shall fail,
and the fields shall yield no meat;
the flock shall be cut off from the fold,
and there shall be no herd in the stalls:
Yet I will rejoice in the Lord,
I will joy in the God of my salvation.
The Lord God is my strength, and he will
make my feet like hinds' feet, and he will
make me to walk upon mine high places.

HABAKKUK 3:17–19

I frequently read about people who have lost all
they love and own. I don't seek out such stories;
this is the way of human life. Natural calamities

and the tragedy of war hit us over and over again. These, combined with the violence and venality of our culture, cause untold grief and loss. Even if you or I escape such catastrophe, we cannot elude the certainty that, at the end of life, all is lost except that which is Christ's. This is why I long to truly learn the secret of the conclusion of Habakkuk.

In his *Complete Commentary on the Whole Bible*, Matthew Henry (1662–1714) is very clear in his understanding of these verses:

> Destroy the vines and the fig-trees, and you make all the mirth of a carnal heart to cease. But those who, when they were full, enjoyed God in all, when they are emptied and impoverished, can enjoy all in God, and can sit down upon a melancholy heap of the ruins of all their creature comforts and even then can sing to the praise and glory of God, as the God of their salvation. This is the principal ground of our joy in God, that he is the God of our salvation, our eternal salvation, the salvation of the

soul; and, if he be so, we may rejoice in him as such in our greatest distresses, since by them our salvation cannot be hindered, but may be furthered.

So I ask, what is the trick to having such godly joy that, if need be, I can "sit down upon a melancholy heap of the ruins of all [my] creature comforts and even then can sing to the praise and glory of God?" I think the secret is found in the prayer recorded in Habakkuk 3:12–19. The God who is revealed in this supplication is unfamiliar to those of us who reside in the age of grace, but it is God nonetheless. Read this prayer and be impressed at how well Habakkuk knows his God and how his language lilts in fluent description of the divine. This is the secret: Know the Lord as well as did Habakkuk. Such knowledge makes your feet like the feet of a deer and enables you to walk upon the heights.

DAY FIFTY-SIX

After this manner therefore pray ye. . .
Give us this day our daily bread.

MATTHEW 6:9, 11

There's an old saying, "Tomorrow never comes." By the time tomorrow arrives, it has become today. All we have to work with is this day; yesterday is gone, and tomorrow never comes. Having said this, I believe the best time to begin to pray for a particular day is just prior to sleep the night before. Evening prayer can help you have a peaceful night's sleep and help you keep the morning watch.

There was a time when cities were safeguarded at night by watchmen who would sound an alarm if danger was near. Then soldiers would muster to protect the citizenry. In ancient Israel there were three watches between sunset and sunrise. In the time of the Roman Empire, there were four. The last watch, which ended at dawn, was called *morning watch*.

I have learned, and you may agree, that real satisfaction is found in the morning watch—a time of prayer before beginning the day's business. I've also found that it is difficult to take this time. I just want to get the day started, yet if I go ahead and do even one thing—make a phone call, check my email, start breakfast—morning watch has passed and the time to pray, "Give us this day our daily bread" has slipped away. I can still stop and pray—we can pray any time of the day—but the morning watch is something special.

Morning watch is a boon to every day. A prayer at night: "Lord, give me grace to arise tomorrow in time to pray," gives your praying spirit the advantage when morning rolls around. God probably likes to answer that request because in morning prayer we are likely to commit our day to God and explain how much we need him to "give us this day our daily bread."

When thou wakest in the morning
 ere thou tread'st the untried way
Of the lot that lies before thee
 through the coming busy day;
Whether sunbeams promise brightness,
 whether dim forebodings fall,
Be thy dawning glad or gloomy,
 go to Jesus, tell him all.

In the calm of sweet communion
 let thy daily work be done;
In the peace of soul-outpouring
 care be banished, patience won;
And if earth with its enchantments
 seek thy spirit to enthrall,
Ere thou listen, ere thou answer,
 turn to Jesus, tell him all.

G. M. Taylor

After this manner therefore pray ye. . .
forgive us our debts,
as we forgive our debtors.

MATTHEW 6:9, 12

Have you heard about the man whose neighbor owed him a few thousand dollars? The man saw his neighbor one day, grabbed him by the throat, and demanded payment. The neighbor fell on his knees and begged for more time to pay. "Be patient and I'll pay," he pleaded. But his creditor wouldn't wait. He had the man jailed until the debt was fully paid.

This story is part of the parable in Matthew 18:23–35. Jesus told this parable in response to a question asked by Peter. " 'Lord, if another member of the church sins against me, how often should I forgive? As many as seven times?' Jesus said to him, 'Not seven times, but, I tell you, seventy-seven times' " (vv. 21–22 NRSV).

Seventy-seven times! Isn't this excessive? To forgive someone once is one time too many by some standards. But should we be afraid of forgiving too much, particularly since we have had unrestrained forgiveness from God? "How often they rebelled against him in the wilderness and grieved him in the desert!" exclaimed the psalmist (Psalm 78:40 NRSV). There is no way to number our sins or know the number of pardons one Christian has received. "[God], being compassionate, forgave their iniquity, and did not destroy them; often he restrained his anger, and did not stir up all his wrath. He remembered that they were but flesh, a wind that passes and does not come again" (vv. 38–39).

The prayer of Matthew 6:12 is frightful. When praying, "Forgive me my debts, as I forgive my debtors," you ask God to treat you as you treat others. In light of this, I think I want God's love to sink into my heart a lot more. Human love has little capacity for forgiveness.

But, as Christians, we can beseech the Lord to teach us the love of Christ that surpasses knowledge so we can "be filled with all the fulness of God." With this we can "be ye kind one to another, tenderhearted, forgiving one another, even as God for Christ's sake hath forgiven [us]" (Ephesians 3:19; 4:32).

After this manner therefore pray ye. . .
And lead us not into temptation,
but deliver us from evil.

MATTHEW 6:9, 13

James wrote, "Let no man say when he is tempted, I am tempted of God: for God cannot be tempted with evil, neither tempteth he any man" (James 1:13). It is important to know this when praying the words of Matthew 6:13. Bible scholars say that the best way to understand this verse is, "Do not allow us to be led into temptation." But there are many temptations. Which one did the Lord mean?

Jesus himself was tempted "in all points. . . like as we are, yet without sin" (Hebrews 4:15).

185

His temptation occurred in three ways during his forty days in the wilderness, which indicates that there are three broad categories of temptation.

First is physical temptation. The devil said, "If thou be the Son of God, command this stone that it be made bread" (Luke 4:3). We need to feed our bodies yet not neglect our soul and spirit. The temptation is to live by bread alone; to only take care of our physical needs. To resist this we must understand "that man shall not live by bread alone, but by every word of God" (v. 4).

Next is moral temptation. The devil showed Jesus all the kingdoms of the world and said, "All this power will I give thee, and the glory of them. . .If thou therefore wilt worship me, all shall be thine" (vv. 5–7). The temptation to seek the world's power and glory is the equivalent of worshipping Satan, so let us pray to "know that we are of God, and the whole world lieth in wickedness" (1 John 5:19).

Finally, there is spiritual temptation. The devil brought Jesus to the top of Jerusalem's temple and said, "If thou be the Son of God, cast thyself down from hence: For it is written, He shall give his angels charge over thee, to keep thee" (Luke 4:9–10). Jesus replied by quoting Deuteronomy 6:16, "Ye shall not tempt the Lord your God," a verse referring to the event at Massah when Israel "tempted the Lord, saying, Is the Lord among us, or not?" (Exodus 17:7). They sought physical evidence of God's care, but "we walk by faith, not by sight" (2 Corinthians 5:7), so let us not be seduced into unbelief by requiring that God prove his love for us.

O Lord, do not let us be led into temptation!

*And, behold, two blind men sitting
by the way side, when they heard that
Jesus passed by, cried out, saying,
Have mercy on us, O Lord,
thou son of David. And the multitude
rebuked them, because they should hold
their peace: but they cried the more,
saying, Have mercy on us, O Lord,
thou son of David. And Jesus stood still,
and called them, and said, What will ye
that I shall do unto you? They say unto
him, Lord, that our eyes may be opened.
So Jesus had compassion on them, and
touched their eyes: and immediately their
eyes received sight, and they followed him.*

MATTHEW 20:30–34

The story that precedes this account of the prayer and healing of the two blind men is also about two men—the disciples James and John. These stories combined teach us about blindness and prayer. In brief, the disciples' story goes like this:

James and John came to Jesus with their mother. She asked the Lord this favor: "In your kingdom, will you let my sons sit in the places of honor next to you?"

"You don't know what you're asking!" Jesus told them. "Are you able to drink from the bitter cup I am about to drink?"

"Oh yes," they replied, "we can do that!"

"True, you'll drink from it," he said. "But only my Father can say who will sit on the thrones next to mine."

The ten other disciples were incensed when they heard what James and John had asked. They probably wanted to sit on those thrones, too. Jesus called them all together and said, "You know that in this world, kings lord it over the people. But among you it should be different. Whoever wants to be your leader must be your servant. Whoever wants to be first must become your slave. Even I came here not to be served but to serve others and give my life as a ransom for many" (Matthew 20:20–29).

Those disciples were blind. They thought that the kingdom operated like the world, that they had an advantage over others and could maneuver their way into positions of authority. They knew nothing about the bitter cup of the cross or how to serve others. This ignorance is spiritual blindness.

There is no record of the disciples' reaction to the Lord's rebuke, but the story of the two blind men tells us how we should respond. Obviously, they knew they were blind. The disciples, on the other hand, were unaware of their own blindness. So let us pray, "Have mercy on me, O Lord, thou son of David, that I would know my own blindness and that my eyes may be opened."

Jesus had compassion on the blind men. Why wouldn't he do the same for us? He touched their eyes, immediately they received sight, and then they followed him. Where was Jesus going? To Jerusalem, to Gethsemane, and to Calvary to drink the bitter cup of suffering.

DAY SIXTY

And he went a little farther,
and fell on his face, and prayed, saying,
O my Father, if it be possible,
let this cup pass from me:
nevertheless not as I will,
but as thou wilt.

MATTHEW 26:39

This is the great Redeemer? This is God become a man? He's sprawled on the ground in an olive orchard, groaning in prayer. Is this what a God-man does?

Yes, this is our God-man Savior. He is revealing his full humanity. He begs that the cup would pass from him, that he might avoid the approaching sufferings. This confirms that

191

he was really and truly human, and, like all of us, he was averse to pain and suffering. The rudimentary factor of the human will is to withdraw from affliction. Christ's reluctance to suffer shows that he was chosen from among men (Hebrews 5:1), is able to sympathize with our weaknesses, and has been tested as we are (4:15).

Note that Jesus calls his sufferings a *cup*. He was given only a cup of suffering—not a river, not an ocean, but a cup. He tipped it to his lips, figuratively speaking, and drank it to the dregs, but not before he asked his Father if it might be possible to avoid its sorrow. That is, if divine justice could be served and God glorified, if humanity could be saved and the creation redeemed, then Jesus would like to be excused. But divine law decreed that this was impossible because "without the shedding of blood there is no forgiveness of sins (Hebrews 9:22 NRSV). Everyone had heard this Jesus say, "My food is to do the will of him who sent me and to complete his work" (John 4:34 NRSV). Thus he prayed three times, "Not what I want but what you want" (Matthew 26:39, 42, 44 NRSV).

Earlier that evening, somewhere in Jerusalem, Jesus Christ had served his disciples supper in an upstairs room. He washed and dried their feet, sat with them, and passed the loaf of bread among them. He also gave them a cup. Jesus said, "This cup is the new covenant in my blood. Do this, as often as you drink it, in remembrance of me" (1 Corinthians 11:25 NRSV). He drank the cup of suffering so that we can drink the cup of blessing. "For as often as you eat this bread and drink the cup, you proclaim the Lord's death until he comes" (v. 26 NRSV).

DAY SIXTY-ONE

And about the ninth hour Jesus cried
with a loud voice, saying,
Eli, Eli, lama sabachthani?
that is to say, My God, my God,
why hast thou forsaken me?

MATTHEW 27:46

The Mississippi River begins its flow to the Gulf
of Mexico as a little gathering of waters away up
north near Grand Rapids, Minnesota. Its vigor
multiplies when joining with Wisconsin's St.
Croix River just south and east of St. Paul. The
Mississippi is a strong, clear current all the way to
its confluence with the Missouri River just north
of St. Louis. At this point it changes.

The Missouri is called the Big Muddy for

good reason. It is thick with silt, the accumulation of its flow through the soils of Montana, North Dakota, South Dakota, Nebraska, Iowa, Kansas, and Missouri. The Mississippi's clear flow meets the Missouri near Alton, Illinois. This conflux creates a Mississippi River that is mighty—a torrent of water collected from ten states—and as brown as all the dirt of the northern plains, the gift of the Big Muddy.

Christ's incredulous prayer, "My God, my God, why hast thou forsaken me?" marks the confluence of the clear flow of God's righteousness with the turbid river of human sin. This is the moment when God made Jesus "to be sin for us, who knew no sin; that we might be made the righteousness of God in him" (2 Corinthians 5:21). Christ's cry marks the end of three hours of midday darkness when the Lamb of God took upon himself the sin of the world (Matthew 27:45; John 1:29). He uttered his anguished query on behalf of darkened humanity, which was ignorant of its answer: "God so loved the world, that he gave his only begotten Son, that whosoever believeth in him should not perish, but have everlasting life" (John 3:16).

Whereas the Missouri muddies the Mississippi, God clarifies humanity. John the Apostle saw "a pure river of water of life, clear as crystal, proceeding out of the throne of God and of the Lamb" (Revelation 22:1). When you believe in Jesus Christ, this river flows into you and becomes "a well of water springing up into everlasting life" (John 4:14). The perfect man, Jesus Christ, prayed, "My God, my God, why hast thou forsaken me?" at the moment he was made sin for us. For the first time in his life, he experienced spiritual thirst (John 19:28). When people believe in him, they are made the righteousness of God and find within themselves the thirst-quenching flow of the water of life (7:37–38).

*The Pharisee stood and prayed
thus with himself, God, I thank thee,
that I am not as other men are,
extortioners, unjust, adulterers,
or even as this publican.
I fast twice in the week,
I give tithes of all that I possess.
And the publican, standing afar off,
would not lift up so much as his eyes unto
heaven, but smote upon his breast, saying,
God be merciful to me a sinner.
I tell you, this man went down
to his house justified rather than the other:
for every one that exalteth himself
shall be abased; and he that humbleth
himself shall be exalted.*

LUKE 18:11–14

My thoughts often come back to these two men, the Pharisee and the tax collector—the self-righteous man of religion and the self-deprecating man of sin. Today I see that the Pharisee isn't actually praying. He boasts to God about his accomplishments and in the same breath criticizes all other men. He sees goodness in himself and badness in others.

The tax collector stands away from the Pharisee. Is he afraid of the religious man's condemnation? Does he think that the Pharisee is right to say that he is an extortioner, unjust, and adulterous? Or maybe he feels his sin so acutely that he's not even thinking about anyone else. One thing is for sure: he knows that he is a sinner. This knowledge fuels genuine prayer.

One of these men knows the Scripture, the other knows the tax code. One occupies a prominent place in the Temple, the other stands at the fringe of the pious gathering. It is good to know the Bible and own an honored place in society, but the Pharisee lacked what the publican possessed, that is, God's light.

Have you ever walked around your neighborhood at night? Some houses have lights on inside and others don't. People in houses with lights on cannot see out into the dark, but a person in a room without light can easily see you walking in the street. The tax collector could not see others' faults because God had enlightened him to his own condition within. The Pharisee was sitting in a darkened room. He could not see himself, but he could see others.

The Pharisee's Bible knowledge was good. His place of honor was good, too. But without a realization of his true condition, these meant nothing. The publican lived on the margins of the Pharisee's world but was enlightened by God. He confessed his sin and went away justified.

"This then is the message which we have heard of him, and declare unto you, that God is light, and in him is no darkness at all. If we say that we have fellowship with him, and walk in darkness, we lie, and do not the truth: But if we walk in the light, as he is in the light, we have fellowship one with another, and the blood of Jesus Christ his Son cleanseth us from all sin" (1 John 1:5–7).

Now is my soul troubled;
and what shall I say?
Father, save me from this hour:
but for this cause came I unto this hour.
Father, glorify thy name.
Then came there a voice from heaven,
saying, I have both glorified it,
and will glorify it again.

JOHN 12:27–28

Jesus Christ often didn't respond to the events of life like the rest of us. He was controlled by purpose, not passion. Here he is standing amidst a throng of people who were among the thousands visiting Jerusalem for the feast of Passover. Many of these had either seen or heard of the resurrection of Lazarus (John 12:17–18). This elevated Jesus to celebrity status in the capital city of the Jews. Even the Pharisees, his enemies, recognized this. They said, "Look, the world has gone after him!" (v. 19 NRSV). People from as far away as Greece were clamoring for his attention (vv. 20–22).

In the midst of an adoring crowd on a sunny day in Jerusalem, Jesus was finally accepted by them all! This would please any one of us, but the soul of Jesus was troubled. Instead of embracing the enthusiasm of the people around him, Jesus accepted God's purpose for his life. He decided against his own glory and prayed, "Father, glorify thy name." This meant that soon Jesus would be nailed to the cross to die for our redemption. Although this troubled him, he knew it was his destiny. A few days later Jesus told his disciples, "Let not your heart be troubled" (14:1). His heart was troubled so that hardship would not trouble our souls. He bore "our sins in his own body on the tree, that we, being dead to sins, should live unto righteousness: by whose stripes ye were healed" (1 Peter 2:24).

Suffering is our destiny, too (1 Thessalonians 3:3), but being healed by his stripes, outward trouble does not spin us into despair. God's name was glorified in Christ's death and resurrection. It is glorified again and again whenever a suffering heart boasts in hope of the glory of God (Romans 5:2).

"And not only so, but we glory in tribulations also: knowing that tribulation worketh patience; And patience, experience; and experience, hope: And hope maketh not ashamed; because the love of God is shed abroad in our hearts by the Holy Ghost which is given unto us. For when we were yet without strength, in due time Christ died for the ungodly" (vv. 3–6).

Neither pray I for these alone,
but for them also which shall believe
on me through their word;
That they all may be one; as thou,
Father, art in me, and I in thee,
that they also may be one in us: that the
world may believe that thou hast sent me.

JOHN 17:20–21

The other day I bought a used car at a small lot in Redmond, Oregon. The salesman there is a Christian and very friendly, as car salesmen often are. As I signed the papers, I gave him a copy of a book I wrote about prayers from the Psalms. He became very quiet, read the back cover, and slowly turned the pages. I got a little nervous.

"Oh, oh," I thought, "he's checking it out for right doctrine." Maybe he was or maybe he wasn't, I don't know. I hope he enjoys reading my book and finds nourishment in a few crumbs of the bread of life that may be there.

I also hope he doesn't find any doctrinal problems. He wouldn't enjoy any food then. That's like trying to eat a salad of unwashed lettuce. Bite one or two grains of sand, and you put down your fork and give it up. This is why, in my writing and in my life, I try to adhere to the common faith (Titus 1:4). The Lord's brother Jude called this the common salvation and said we should contend for this faith "which was once delivered unto the saints" (Jude 1:3). Despite the different teachings and practices that exist among Christians, we share the same faith and salvation, just as we have the same Lord. Through these truths Jesus' prayer for oneness can be fulfilled.

The apostle Paul reminds us "of the good news that I proclaimed to you, which you in turn received, in which also you stand, through which also you are being saved" (1 Corinthians 15:1–2 NRSV). He said that the following are of first importance: "That Christ died for our sins in accordance with the scriptures, and that he was buried, and that he was raised on the third day in accordance with the scriptures" (vv. 3–4 NRSV).

We stand together in a faith founded only on Christ; his death, his life, and his resurrection, as revealed in the Bible. Other Christian customs and teachings may be good or right or seemingly necessary, but they are not part of the faith that allows our common salvation. Paul fought the good fight of this faith (1 Timothy 6:12), and he earnestly issued this warning: "As we have said before, so now I repeat, if anyone proclaims to you a gospel contrary to what you received, let that one be accursed!" (Galatians 1:9 NRSV).

*O righteous Father, the world hath
not known thee: but I have known thee,
and these have known that thou hast
sent me. And I have declared unto them
thy name, and will declare it:
that the love wherewith thou hast
loved me may be in them, and I in them.*

JOHN 17:25–26

My father and I shared the same name—Daniel.
His colleagues and friends called him Dan,
though he had one good friend who called him
Dan'l. Only my sisters and I could call him Dad,
because he had begotten us. We were his
children. We were born of him. Although my
dad has passed away, I am still very close to him.

I remember him. I know a lot about his life. But he does not just live in my memories; much more so, he lives deep within me. This is not because I am exactly like him, but because he gave me physical life. His life is in me. Although I inherited some of his bodily and psychological attributes, there is something deeper and inexplicable about my relationship with him. All I can say is, he is my father.

So it is with God. Only those who are born of God can call him Father. This is the divine name that Jesus Christ declared to us. When Jesus told Mary Magdalene, "I ascend unto my Father, and your Father" (John 20:17), he was indicating that, because of his death and resurrection, the relationship of humanity with divinity had changed. God would no longer be entirely objective, far away from us in heaven. Instead, simply by believing, people could be born of God and, spiritually speaking, share the divine life.

Jesus said, "That which is born of the flesh is flesh; and that which is born of the Spirit is spirit" (John 3:6). My flesh is born of my physical father, Dan Partner, and in many ways

I am just like him. Likewise, my spirit is born of God's Spirit, and so I have inherited aspects of the divine life. I know God's name is Father.

This is very difficult to understand. Nicodemus was the first man to hear that he could be born of God (vv. 3–8), and, despite his education and wisdom, all Nicodemus could say was, "How can these things be?" (v. 9). The Bible, which is devoted to deciphering this wonder, explains our experience in this way, "You have received a spirit of adoption. When we cry, 'Abba! Father!' it is that very Spirit bearing witness with our spirit that we are children of God" (Romans 8:15–16 NRSV).

And they stoned Stephen,
calling upon God, and saying, Lord Jesus,
receive my spirit. And he kneeled down,
and cried with a loud voice,
Lord, lay not this sin to their charge.
And when he had said this,
he fell asleep.

ACTS 7:59–60

Imagine the fury and tumult that surrounded Stephen on the day he died. "They became enraged and ground their teeth at Stephen. . . . They covered their ears, and with a loud shout all rushed together against him. Then they dragged him out of the city and began to stone him" (Acts 7:54, 57–58 NRSV). Human life is powerful. It is not easy to kill. The Welsh poet Dylan Thomas said it well: We "do not go gentle into that good night." How much effort did it take to kill Stephen? How many stones did they throw?

It took the power of a full-blown riot to accomplish the martyrdom of Stephen. But Stephen was a full-blown Christian. He was "a man full of faith and the Holy Spirit. . .full of grace and power (6:5, 8 NRSV). Stephen had become such a person in part because he was immersed in the Scriptures. With eloquence and insight, he had expounded the history of Israel (7:2–53). It was spiritual nourishment that made him what he was. Stephen truly knew that "one does not live by bread alone," (Luke 4:4 NRSV).

No doubt Stephen was experienced in prayer. Amidst this murderous melee, he prayed very similar words to those his Lord had uttered on the cross, "Lord Jesus, receive my spirit" (Psalm 31:5; Luke 23:46). But this was not his final prayer. Stephen's heart had been so expanded by the love of God that his last thought was not of himself. He knelt as if to emphasize the importance of his supplication. Then he shouted out a prayer of forgiveness that anyone whose soul has been hurt or offended should repeat with equal fervor: "Lord, do not hold this sin against them" (Acts 7:60 NRSV).

Surrounded by chaos and robbed of his life, Stephen was at peace. He simply fell asleep until the day when, "in the twinkling of an eye, at the last trump. . .the dead shall be raised incorruptible" (v. 60; 1 Corinthians 15:52).

Who art thou, Lord?

ACTS 22:8

One day Paul asked a question that would change him forever: "Who are you, Lord?" If everyone, including Christians, would ask God this question, the world would be much improved. We would know God and ourselves much better. The answer Paul received shows that God is in no way partial to a person's position in human society (Galatians 2:6).

Among the Jews of Jerusalem, Paul had reason to be most confident. He was "a member of the people of Israel, of the tribe of Benjamin, a Hebrew born of Hebrews; as to the law, a Pharisee; as to zeal, a persecutor of the church; as to righteousness under the law, blameless" (Philippians 3:5–6 NRSV). He was born in Tarsus, which is across the Mediterranean Sea from the land of Israel. But he showed such promise and zeal for God that he was sent to Jerusalem to study with Gamaliel, who educated Paul strictly according to the ancestral law of the Jews. The young man was well known by the high priest and the council of elders. No doubt Paul's star was rising among the religious leaders in Jerusalem (Acts 22:3–5).

Yet the Lord didn't tell Paul, "I am the God of your fathers." He didn't say the words a leading Jew would hope for: "I am the God of Abraham, Isaac, and Jacob" (see Exodus 3:6). Rather, the Lord said, "I am Jesus of Nazareth" (Acts 22:8). To Paul's sophisticated ear this meant that the Lord was a lawless man from a hick town. Only a few years before, this Jesus had been executed as a criminal, but now he was speaking out of a great light from heaven (Acts 22:6–7).

Paul asked, "Who are you, Lord?" and received the revelation of Jesus Christ. "For his sake," the apostle later wrote, "I have suffered the loss of all things, and I regard them as rubbish, in order that I may gain Christ and be found in him, not having a righteousness of my own that comes from the law, but one that comes through faith in Christ" (Philippians 3:8–9 NRSV).

"Who are you, Lord?" is a powerful prayer.

*Now the God of patience and consolation
grant you to be likeminded one toward
another according to Christ Jesus:
That ye may with one mind and one
mouth glorify God, even the Father of
our Lord Jesus Christ. Wherefore receive
ye one another, as Christ also received
us to the glory of God.*

ROMANS 15:5–7

The following is the consoling phrase that
begins the book of 2 Corinthians: "Blessed
be God, even the Father of our Lord Jesus
Christ, the Father of mercies, and the God of
all comfort" (1:3). What a beautiful God this
is! Could a Father of mercies be cruel? Does the

God of all comfort cause distress? I say no, no.

In the above prayer from Romans, Paul prays to this God, the God of patience and consolation. He implores that we Christians would be like-minded toward one another according to Christ. He wants God to give us the ability to live together in harmony because we follow Jesus. In other words, he asks that we worshippers become like the one we adore—our patient and encouraging God.

This is possible because God is our Father. We who believe in Jesus Christ are God's children; we share the divine life, which is patient and encouraging. If each of us would draw from this well of eternal life, we could easily be like-minded toward one another, with one mind and one mouth glorify God and fulfill the apostle's prayer.

Does this sound like a dream? Am I preaching a pie-in-the-sky gospel of Christian harmony? All I know is that I long for the God of all comfort, the Father of mercies, and pray that God be glorified among all Christians. This is possible. Romans 15:7 gives us a practical way to express the Father's love—"Receive ye one another, as Christ also received us to the glory of God."

Christ freely welcomed each of us, the lost sheep, into his fold to feed among the flock of God (Luke 19:10). Even more, we are members of his family (Romans 8:29). Beyond this, we are betrothed as the bride of Christ (Ephesians 5:25; Revelation 19:7). Should we be so unkind to those that are his? No. Do you pray the Lord's Prayer? Have you forgiven others to the extent that Christ has forgiven you? This is the way to glorify the Father of mercies.

"Bear with one another and, if anyone has a complaint against another, forgive each other; just as the Lord has forgiven you, so you also must forgive" (Colossians 3:13 NRSV).

But thanks be to God, who in Christ always leads us in triumphal procession, and through us spreads in every place the fragrance that comes from knowing him.

2 CORINTHIANS 2:14 NRSV

In the days when Rome was conquering the world, great processions commemorated the return of its victorious armies, during which the victors paraded their captives before the emperor and his court. Paul celebrates a similar procession in the thanksgiving prayer recorded in 2 Corinthians 2:14. Here, the apostle Paul is a prisoner of Christ Jesus (Ephesians 3:1; 4:1) and sees himself being led in triumph in the Lord's victory parade.

The Romans hung garlands and scattered flowers about as their parades progressed. Incense was burned as the soldiers and their prisoners passed through the streets. So Paul, continuing his analogy, says, "we are the aroma of Christ to God among those who are being saved and among those who are perishing" (2 Corinthians 2:15 NRSV).

Sometimes people know I am a Christian even though I've never mentioned it to them. The only way I can account for this is through the above verses in 2 Corinthians. Christ must be spreading the aroma of his victory parade. People don't smell this with their nose; they apparently sense it in their heart.

Why was Paul a prisoner of the Lord? Am I his prisoner for the same reason? If so, then I am really in his aromatic parade.

The apostle Paul brought the gospel to the non-Jewish people of the world, and this is what he preached: "Now in Christ Jesus you who once were far off [from God] have been brought near by the blood of Christ. For he is our peace; in his flesh he has made both groups into one and has broken down the dividing wall, that is, the hostility between us" (Ephesians 2:13, 14 NRSV). A person who comprehends God's love in the gospel of Jesus Christ sees others as God does. That is, there is no difference between us except that some people have believed in Jesus and some people have not yet believed in him. Nevertheless, God loved everyone in the world and gave them his only begotten Son (John 3:16).

Paul was imprisoned for realizing and preaching these things (Ephesians 3:1). When a person understands the gospel, he or she becomes its captive. This captivity is accompanied by a spiritual fragrance spread by Christ. I find this astounding. As Paul said, "Who is sufficient for these things?" (2 Corinthians 2:16).

DAY SEVENTY

*That the God of our Lord Jesus Christ,
the Father of glory, may give unto you
the spirit of wisdom and revelation
in the knowledge of him:
The eyes of your understanding being
enlightened; that ye may know what
is the hope of his calling, and what [are]
the riches of the glory of his inheritance
in the saints, And what is the exceeding
greatness of his power to us-ward
who believe, according to the working
of his mighty power.*

EPHESIANS 1:17–19

I don't know what to say about this prayer. Can I
explain the spirit of wisdom and revelation? No.

All I can say is that it imparts the knowledge of the Father of glory. Can anything I write enlighten the eyes of your understanding or let you know what is the hope of God's calling or what are the riches of the glory of God's inheritance in the saints? No. Who can describe the exceeding greatness of God's power toward those who believe? No one.

Even the apostle Paul doesn't explain these things. He was caught up to the third heaven and into Paradise and heard things that no mortal is permitted to repeat (2 Corinthians 12:2–4). He wrote much of the New Testament, yet he does not attempt to explain the inexplicable. Instead, having "heard of your faith in the Lord Jesus and your love toward all the saints," he remembered you in his prayers (Ephesians 1:15–16): "That the God of our Lord Jesus Christ, the Father of glory, may give unto you the spirit of wisdom and revelation in the knowledge of him: The eyes of your understanding being enlightened; that ye may know what is the hope of his calling, and what [are] the riches of the glory of his inheritance in the saints, And what is the exceeding greatness of his power to us-ward who believe, according to the working of his mighty power" (vv. 17–19).

Isn't this truly what you want? The knowledge of him, the hope of his calling, the riches of his inheritance in the saints, the greatness of his power? I doubt there is a more important prayer than this and urge you to every day make Paul's prayer your own. This is how it goes: "Oh God of my Lord Jesus Christ, Father of glory, give me the spirit of wisdom and revelation in the knowledge of yourself. Enlighten the eyes of my understanding so that I can know what is the hope of your calling, and what are the riches of the glory of your inheritance in the saints, and what is the exceeding greatness of your power to me and all those who believe according to the working of your mighty power."

Amen.

DAY SEVENTY-ONE

*That he would grant you,
according to the riches of his glory,
to be strengthened with might
by his Spirit in the inner man;
That Christ may dwell in your hearts by
faith; that ye, being rooted and grounded
in love, May be able to comprehend with
all saints what is the breadth, and length,
and depth, and height; and to know the
love of Christ, which passeth knowledge,
that ye might be filled with
all the fulness of God.*

EPHESIANS 3:16–19

This is the companion prayer to the one in Ephesians 1:17–19. Instead of physical strength, which is so desirable to us all, this prayer seeks strength for the inner man. Instead of your own established dwelling place, this prayer asks that Christ may have a home in your heart and that your roots would be in God's love. While we pray for one thing—our home or our health—the Lord is interested in something else. Jesus is again saying to us, "Foxes have holes, and birds of the air have nests; but the Son of man hath not where to lay his head" (Luke 9:58).

This prayer asks about travel, too. People love to travel. Dozens of elaborate recreational vehicles pass through my town every day in the spring, summer, and fall. If you were to ask and God were to answer the prayer of Ephesians 3, you would be traveling the breadth, and length, and depth, and height of "a better country, that is, an heavenly" (Hebrews 11:16).

Sometimes I feel lonely and unloved. Do you? This prayer has this covered, too. It asks that you would "know the love of Christ, which passeth knowledge." This love abolishes loneliness. What about possessions? Surely we need material possessions, but it is equally true that material possessions do not satisfy our souls. So this prayer asks that you be filled with all the fulness of God.

No one should fear to pray the prayer of Ephesians 3:16–19. By seeking strength for your inner man, you don't run the risk of weakening your body. If Christ could find a comfortable home in your heart, I doubt that you would find yourself homeless. Those who follow the way of Abraham, the father of faith, confess "that they were strangers and pilgrims on the earth." Aren't we eager to travel to the city God has prepared for us? (Hebrews 11:13, 16). So let's be bold to pray according to this prayer so that one day we all will be filled to overflowing with God.

DAY SEVENTY-TWO

Be careful for nothing;
but in every thing by prayer and
supplication with thanksgiving let
your requests be made known unto God.
And the peace of God, which passeth all
understanding, shall keep your hearts
and minds through Christ Jesus.

PHILIPPIANS 4:6–7

Think of the billions of people who have passed across the face of the earth since Paul wrote this advice about prayer. Each person had problems and was tied-in tight with other people. The complexity of human society is incomprehensible. Yet the scripture presents everyone with the same advice: Don't worry about anything;

instead, give thanks and pray. This is amazing. What's more, an answer is guaranteed, though it is not what those billions may have expected. Instead of a direct response to the requests of prayer, God gives a praying person divine peace through Christ.

This promise echoes the words of Jesus: "Peace I leave with you, my peace I give unto you: not as the world giveth, give I unto you. Let not your heart be troubled, neither let it be afraid" (John 14:27). By saying, "Not as the world giveth, give I unto you," Jesus meant that these are not mere words. His promise of peace is not like a platitude in a greeting card. This is real.

Though the peace of God is beyond our understanding, it is not beyond our experience. It is as real as God is real. God is the God of peace who will "crush Satan under your feet" (Romans 16:20 NRSV), "a God not of disorder but of peace" (1 Corinthians 14:33 NRSV), who gives you "peace at all times in all ways" (2 Thessalonians 3:16 NRSV) and sanctifies you entirely (1 Thessalonians 5:23).

We Christians believe in "the God of peace,

who brought back from the dead our Lord Jesus, the great shepherd of the sheep, by the blood of the eternal covenant" (Hebrews 13:20 NRSV). There is one little thing that we must do to experience this God of peace, and that is pray. Nothing more is asked of us. "In every thing by prayer and supplication with thanksgiving let your requests be made known unto God. And the peace of God, which passeth all understanding, shall keep your hearts and minds through Christ Jesus" (Philippians 4:6–7).

*And the very God of peace
sanctify you wholly; and I pray God
your whole spirit and soul and body
be preserved blameless unto the
coming of our Lord Jesus Christ.
Faithful is he that calleth you,
who also will do it.*

1 THESSALONIANS 5:23–24

The apostle Paul begins his epistle to the believers in Thessalonica by assuring them that he always gives thanks "to God for all of you and mention you in our prayers, constantly" (1 Thessalonians 1:2 NRSV). His prayer at the end of this letter tells the substance of his hopes for the believers: "and I pray God your whole spirit and soul and body be preserved blameless unto the coming of our Lord Jesus Christ" (1 Thessalonians 5:23).

Paul sure aimed high, didn't he? He wouldn't settle for anything less than holiness in every part of every believer in Christ. His aim was that God would "so strengthen your hearts in holiness that you may be blameless before our God and Father at the coming of our Lord Jesus with all his saints" (3:13 NRSV).

Jesus Christ is coming back. In this light, the utter holiness of Christ's believers is not an unreasonable expectation. What is unreasonable to expect is that we, the believers, would bear the responsibility for such complete sanctification. Note that in 1 Thessalonians 5:23, Paul asks *God* to preserve us blameless. The same is true in 3:13. There, God will strengthen our hearts in holiness. But this does not mean that we can be passive. Just as plants receive sunlight and rain and nourishment from the soil in order to grow, so must we be open to God's light and nourishment from the Word and remain rooted in his divine love. Still, let's rejoice in the fact that it is God who gives us the growth (1 Corinthians 3:7 NRSV). In other words, let's take pleasure in doing what is necessary to grow in Christ and allow Christ to grow in us. For this, James gives good advice: "Be patient, therefore, beloved, until the coming of the Lord. The farmer waits for the precious crop from the earth, being patient with it until it receives the early and the late rains. You also must be patient. Strengthen your hearts, for the coming of the Lord is near" (James 5:7–8 NRSV).

*I thank my God, making mention
of thee always in my prayers,
Hearing of thy love and faith,
which thou hast toward the Lord Jesus,
and toward all saints.*

PHILEMON 1:4–5

Isn't this a touching prayer? The old man Paul was in trouble and in the custody of Roman authorities (Philemon 1:9). Yet he doesn't pray about his troubles and difficulties. He's just happy to have Philemon as a friend in Christ, so he gives thanks to God for him and often prays for him.

We frequently pray about our troubles and personal tragedies—rightly so. Paul says that we should make our requests known to God (Philippians 4:6). But the apostle himself doesn't do this very much. The record of his epistles shows that he mostly prayed for others. Paul told Timothy that he constantly remembered him in prayer (2 Timothy 1:3). To the Romans he testified "that without ceasing I make mention of you always in my prayers" (Romans 1:9). The Thessalonians, Philippians, Ephesians, and Colossians were also beneficiaries of Paul's supplications to God (1 Thessalonians 1:2; Philippians 1:3–4; Ephesians 1:16; Colossians 1:9).

In Romans 16 you'll find the names of some of the people for whom Paul prayed. This lively chapter gives a glimpse into the life of the church in Rome with its families and fellow-workers, converts, and others. There's the beloved Epaenetus, the first convert in Achaia, and Andronicus and Junia, who were in prison with Paul and prominent among the apostles. There are Herodion, Narcissus, and Rufus, and many more. All these people are colors and brush strokes in a beautiful painting of the church in Rome.

This chapter also shows the effect of prayer on Paul's heart. He lovingly greets so many people. They are all beloved to him. Paul must have met many of these brothers and sisters during his travels in Asia and visits to Jerusalem, because at the time he wrote the epistle to the Romans, he had not yet visited Rome. Though he may not have seen these folks for years, he hadn't forgotten them. Prayer for others engraves their names on our hearts and enlarges them so we can care for more than simply our own affairs.

To pray as Paul did brings peace into the church. This is why the apostle was assured that "the God of peace shall bruise Satan under your feet shortly" (Romans 16:20). Let's all pray like this more and more so we can with sincerity say to our fellow believers, "The grace of our Lord Jesus Christ be with you" (v. 20).

Day Seventy-Five

He which testifieth these things saith,
Surely I come quickly. Amen.
Even so, come, Lord Jesus.

Revelation 22:20

When I was a young believer, I belonged to a church that made the second coming of Christ into a frightful thing for believers. The ministers used the Lord's parables and teachings in such a way that I feared I would not be ready when the Lord returned. Although most of their teachings were very good, I was taught that I had to have a certain level of Christian growth and commitment in order to be considered an overcomer in the last day. I now know that these teachers misrepresented the truth for the purpose of controlling the church's members through fear.

Mercifully the Lord helped me find a way out of that congregation. But it took me some time to rid myself of a residual dread of the Lord's return. One day I was standing under the oak tree in my front yard. It was a clear summer day, and the breeze was gently blowing my children's rope swing in the tree. I said, "Lord, I don't care what happens to me when you come back. All I know is that then this world will be an infinitely better place. So come, Lord Jesus." That prayer healed me of the fear.

The Second Coming of Christ is a big mystery. It is hard to know exactly what will happen at the end of the age. The Scriptures describe this event in various ways, but not to invoke fear in our hearts. Instead, we are to "encourage one another with these words" (1 Thessalonians 4:18 NRSV) and together tirelessly invoke the Bible's final prayer, "Amen. Even so, come, Lord Jesus" (Revelation 22:20).

The church looks for the Lord's return like a bride awaiting her bridegroom. We love him and he loves us, so we sing:

The voice of my beloved!
Look, he comes,
leaping upon the mountains,
bounding over the hills.
My beloved is like a gazelle
or a young stag. . .
My beloved speaks and says to me:

"Arise, my love, my fair one,
and come away;
for now the winter is past,
the rain is over and gone.
The flowers appear on the earth;
the time of singing has come,
and the voice of the turtledove
is heard in our land."

Song of Solomon 2:8–12 NRSV

ABOUT THE AUTHOR

Daniel Partner lives on the southern Oregon coast with his wife Margaret, a storyteller, and son Jeb. He can be reached by E-mail at author@danpartner.com.

Other Inspirational Library Books by Daniel Partner

The Story of Jesus: A Portrait of Christ from the Bible—The biblical accounts of the life and teachings of Jesus Christ from the gospels of Matthew, Mark, Luke, and John are assembled in this book into one easy-to-read chronological story. Includes a complete outline of the Lord's life. A wonderful tool for understanding the Bible $4.99

I Give Myself to Prayer: Devotional Thoughts on Prayers from the Psalms—The devotional thoughts that accompany these seventy-five prayers collected from the book of Psalms make them as meaningful in our lives today as they were in the times of Moses, Solomon, and David $4.99

Peace Like a River: Devotional Thoughts of Comfort from Classic Christian Hymns—Forty classic hymns, both well known and less familiar, are the basis for these contemporary devotional selections which help you turn your eyes upon Jesus, the source of all true peace $4.99

The Inspirational Library is a series of beautiful purse/pocket-size editions of Christian classics bound in flexible leatherette. These books make thoughtful gifts for everyone on your list, including yourself!

Available wherever books are sold.
Or order from:

Barbour Publishing, Inc.
P.O. Box 719
Uhrichsville, OH 44683
www.barbourbooks.com

If you order by mail, add $2.00 to your order for shipping.
Prices are subject to change without notice.